W9-CTI-774

The
Edge of
Fire

The Edge of Fire

Volcano and Earthquake Country in Western North America and Hawaii

text and photographs by
Robert Wenkam

SIERRA CLUB BOOKS   San Francisco

The Sierra Club, founded in 1892 by John Muir, has devoted itself to the study and protection of the earth's scenic and ecological resources—mountains, wetlands, woodlands, wild shores and rivers, deserts and plains. The publishing program of the Sierra Club offers books to the public as a nonprofit educational service in the hope that they may enlarge the public's understanding of the Club's basic concerns. The point of view expressed in each book, however, does not necessarily represent that of the Club. The Sierra Club has some sixty chapters coast to coast, in Canada, Hawaii, and Alaska. For information about how you may participate in its programs to preserve wilderness and the quality of life, please address inquiries to Sierra Club, 730 Polk Street, San Francisco, CA 94109.

Jacket design by Bonnie Smetts
Book design by Bonnie Smetts
Printed by Dai Nippon Printing Company, Ltd., Tokyo, Japan
10 9 8 7 6 5 4 3 2 1

Library of Congress Cataloging-in-Publication Data

Wenkam, Robert, 1920–
    The edge of fire.

    Bibliography: p. 160
    1. Volcanoes—Pacific Coast (North America)
2. Volcanoes—Hawaii. I. Title.
QE524.W45 1987 551.2′1′0979   87-4431
ISBN 0-87156-714-8

For my children, living with us all on the edge of fire:
Chiye, Miyo, Jay, Tad.

Civilization exists by geological consent, subject to change without notice.

WILL DURANT

Contents

Foreword

Most of us are vaguely aware that the face of our planet has changed repeatedly in the past—that mountains have risen and faded away, that the seas have come and gone across the land, and that volcanic activity was once involved in the formation of the primordial earth. But those obscure concepts seem somehow distant in human terms, and we go about our requisite daily tasks of life, confident that the earth beneath our feet will continue to provide support.

Our faith in the permanence of the earth is misplaced if we extrapolate that confidence too far into the future. The Earth's crust is a dynamic, fragile platform, and nowhere is the fragility of that platform more demonstrable than on the rim of the Pacific Ocean, where the shape of the land is literally changing every day, and where the potential for devastatingly rapid change is an inevitable factor to be ignored only at society's peril.

The Island of Hawaii provides an ideal vantage point to contemplate the ephemeral nature of the earth beneath our feet, owing to the frequency with which the face of the land changes. Late one evening last month I spent an incredible few hours along a remote part of the Kalapana coast sharing a large fresh water pond with a molten flow of *pahoehoe* lava. The flow was gently cascading into my private sauna, gradually boiling away and displacing the water. I could choose any temperature from cool to boiling, depending on how close I swam to the flow. The scene was illuminated by a soft red-orange light from the flow and background music was provided by the hissing and booming interaction of fire and water. "Now, what would the California hot tub crowd think about *this*," I wondered? As the pond became smaller and the water hotter I found a platform of smooth stones at one end on which I could recline above the water. The contours of the platform fit my body perfectly and I realized they had been assembled by the hands of Hawaiian sunbathers long ago. Resting on those ancient stones I thought of my place on this fast-changing land and of the ebb and flow of man, fire, and earthquakes on this very spot. The ponds had been formed by presumably sudden down-dropping of the coastal land beneath the water table during some prehistoric earthquake a few hundred years ago. The lava flow on which the ponds developed was itself less than a thousand years old, and had buried an earlier-occupied area, as indicated by the molds of man-introduced coconut palms frozen in the rock. So, people had settled this area, been forced away by a lava flow, experienced an earthquake which formed the ponds, had used the ponds for their pleasure, and were now being driven away again. Nonetheless, man had counted his losses, adapted to the new shape of the land, and life had gone on. Two hours before my swim in the pond I had documented the burning of my friend Louie Pau's home for insurance purposes before it had been engulfed by lava. Louie and his wife lost their home, beautiful gardens, and most of their belongings but when I saw them a few days later they showed the Hawaiian adaptability that has evolved so well in this land of change: "Well, we'll rebuild when *Pele* is pau—our land is still there, just changed."

Life on this Earth has evolved in concert with, and in large part because of, geologic change, and all life has a built-in capacity for adjustment to catastrophic change. So if you live on *The Edge of Fire*, take heart—the diversity and beauty of the landscape and life around you is a direct product of the earth forces beneath your feet. Enjoy the vitality of your surroundings, and feel a bit of pity for those who reside in continental heartlands where the hills stay the same for tens of millions of years. How *boring* it must be for those folks!

John P. Lockwood, Geologist
Volcano, Hawaii
January 1987

Acknowledgments

Chasing volcanoes is routine for islanders living in Hawaii, where Kilauea, by some accounts, is the most active volcano in the world. The late Dr. Gordon A. MacDonald, volcanologist and university professor, first introduced me to the excitement and drama of the earth erupting. We hiked Hawaii Island from top to bottom. He warned me away from toxic fumes in Puna volcanic vents and actually pulled me out of a lava tube when the thin roof collapsed beneath my feet as we walked across a fresh pahoehoe lava flow within Mauna Loa's summit caldera of Mokuaweoweo. We had often talked about working together on this book.

Over the years, many others have helped me understand our drifting earth and volcanic activity on every continent. Gordon Morse, a longtime resident on the slopes of Kilauea (his post-office box is at Volcano), has helped me gain access to all sorts of remote places. Together we watched Kapoho Town burn and then be buried beneath Puna lava during a most exciting night of volcano watching.

Others have read my words at my request, often correcting facts, and as often disagreeing with my personal conclusions, but the final text is my responsibility and over their objections incorporates many of my own ideas about the shaking earth and why it looks the way it does and what might happen: Gene Foushee, geologist and owner-builder of Recapture Lodge in Bluff, Utah; Norm Banks, USGS, Vancouver, Washington; Jack Lockwood, USGS, Hawaii Volcano Observatory, Hawaii Volcanoes National Park; Loraine Carlson, Chicago, author of the best guidebooks to Mexico and Maya country; Herb Luthin, editor, Chicago, who made so many of my early words read well; and Sherilyn Mentes, whose reminders of closely approaching deadlines were always quite important.

There is my typist, Toba Wheeler of Irvine, California. Those who put me up for the night: Carol Ann Davis, bed and breakfast, Koloa, Kauai; Sheraton Hotels of Hawaii; Kona Village Resort; El Camino Real Westin Hotel, Mexico City; The Inn of the Seventh Mountain and Sunriver, Bend, Oregon; Lee and Cal Wilson, Makawao, Maui; The Maui Connection, Maui; and Timberline Mountain Guides, Terrebonne, Oregon. Martin Litton kindly flew me over the full length of the San Andreas fault.

And there were many helpful people I met along the way from El Salvador to Alaska, from Wyoming to Hawaii, along the edge of the North American continental plate, people whose names I cannot remember, but whose kindness and hospitality I shall not forget.

CHAPTER ONE

The Hillside on Huehue Ranch

Halemaumau firepit, Kilauea caldera, Hawaii.

High on Hawaii's cloud-shrouded north slope of Hualalai, not far above the narrow belt road winding interminably between the Kona coast and Waimea town, is located a most unusual hole in the ground. The hole is solidly plugged at present, but about the time of Captain Cook's arrival in the islands the gaping vent opened in the earth's crust, spewing a fountain of molten rock that flowed swiftly to the sea. It covered cultivated Hawaiian *kuleanas* along the shore and formed long, wriggling strings of lava that are a characteristic feature of the now dormant Hualalai volcano, as well as its still very active neighbor, Mauna Loa.

The lava was unusually thin, possibly the consistency of sugarcane molasses, and discharged with such rapidity from the molten interior of the earth that fragments of the earth's mantle many miles below the crust broke loose from the conduit's fractured wall and were swept quickly to the surface without melting into the basaltic lava.

Composed of almost pure minerals—iron and magnesium combined with silica—the black, heavy rock fragments did not become part of the lava mix flowing from the volcanic vent. The viscous magma drained away, leaving extremely dense rocks from deep within the earth scattered about the vent; these settled out of the molten lava like stones do when dropping to the bottom of a riverbed as floodwaters reach a still pool.

Like few other places in the world, this isolated hillside on Huehue Ranch in upper Kona is littered with rare specimens of the earth's interior. The strange-looking heavy rocks are out of place among the familiar *pahoehoe* and *aa* basaltic lavas. To pick one up is to grasp a peculiarly heavy weight, for it is considerably denser than ordinary surface rocks. Smash one open, if you can, and expose a glimpse of the inner earth—the beautiful glitter of a primordial semiprecious stone.

It is a kimberlite diatreme, in which diamonds are sometimes found, a volcanic pipe that opened up from depths probably in excess of 100 miles below the surface crust, over a century ago. Exploding to the surface at three times the speed of sound, it is one of the more spectacular geological phenomena known.

A close-up look into the earth's hot interior is possible at Kilauea in Hawaii, where magma continues to extrude in fountains of molten rock as it has for many millions of years while creating the Hawaiian Islands, one by one, as the earth's crust in the mid-Pacific drifted slowly northward, then to the northwest. A line of seamounts and islands over 5,000 miles long, beginning below the surface south of the Alaskan Aleutians, rising above the sea at Midway and continuing south, delineates the path of the earth's drifting crust—the Pacific tectonic plate—as the seabed and protruding islands slide northwest at the rate of about 4 inches a year. The molten interior of the earth, kept hot by the decay of radioactive elements—mainly uranium, thorium, and potassium—is trapped by the insulating mantle, which sometimes cracks, releasing magma to ooze onto the surface, pushing underwater mountains through the crust as the seabed slides over the hot spot in the ocean floor, forming islands at sea level and seamounts below. Some 20 miles south of the present Big Island of Hawaii is the newest island, still a seamount, estimated to reach the surface in about 10,000 years. The undersea volcano, already named Loihi, is now within 3,000 feet of the surface.

The Hawaiian Islands are dramatic evidence of the power of nature, and its beauty summons visitors from around the world. In Hawaii's gentle volcanoes the distant origins of many of earth's landforms are graphically revealed. Hawaii's eruptions accurately accept the description of "drive-in" volcanoes, where the National Park Service has built a 200-car paved parking lot on *pahoehoe* lava, not 50

Kilauea Iki eruption, Hawaii Volcanoes National Park, Hawaii.

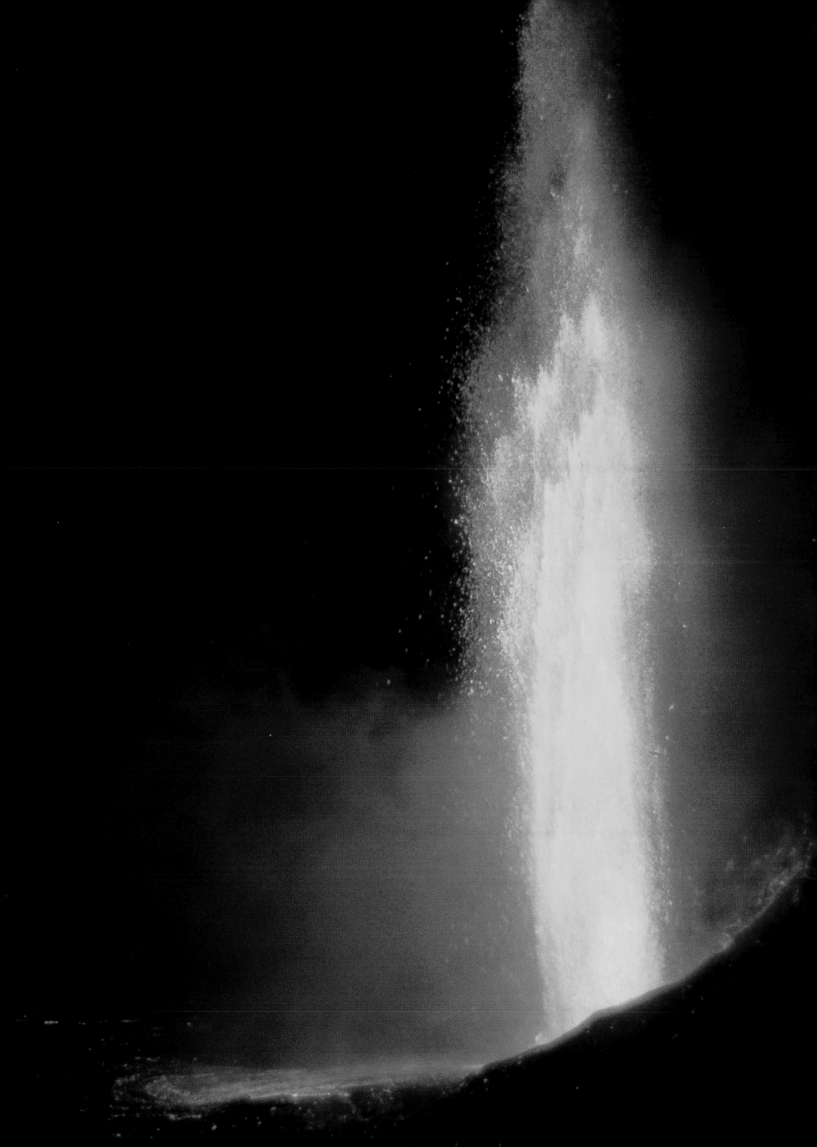

yards from the rim of collapsing Halemaumau firepit within Kilauea's caldera. It is the end of the road for a million visitors a year and a popular destination for island residents and tourists who swarm like bugs to a pheromone to watch Kilauea put on a show. The volcano has its own telephone number (808/967-7977) at Park Service headquarters, where taped announcements of harmonic quakes indicating lava movement and best viewing locations are available for visitors who never fear a close inspection of the earth's fiery splendors. Kilauea has no danger zone as does Mt. St. Helens. In Hawaii an eruption notice is not a warning but an announcement for the tourist industry to prepare for the rush.

SOME 4,000 MILES from Hawaii is another famed hot spot on the earth's crust, this one in midcontinent on the North American plate where the famous geysers and hot fumaroles of Yellowstone National Park are main-

tained over a volcanic plume in the mantle.

The North American crust creeps slowly westward, edging past the Grand Teton fault at Yellowstone on a granite hinge, sliding around and over its own hot spot. Molten magma lies not much more than two miles beneath portions of the collapsed ancient Yellowstone caldera, bulging upward at the rate of one-half inch each year. The last major volcanic eruption in the area occurred 600,000 years ago when the place was relatively new. Should an eruption occur again, Old Faithful geyser would undoubtedly change its performance schedule, and if past volcanic activity can be taken as any indication of the future, a dozen western states may be buried in hot ash, blown from a new volcano erupting from the intersection of three major fault zones in Yellowstone.

One of these faults extends directly south into the Tetons, a geologically young and still-growing range of mountains. The Teton eastern front—standing bold across the skyline, a jagged granite wall when viewed from the

West Thumb geyser area in winter, Yellowstone National Park, Wyoming.

Norris Geyser Basin, Yellowstone National Park, Wyoming.

Snake River overlook made famous by Ansel Adams photographs—is the result of a continuous if intermittent upthrust of more than 20,000 feet on a steeply inclined fracture beginning below the present surface. The visual effect is spectacular and may be even more so in another hundred years as the Tetons continue growing higher and Yellowstone grows hotter.

The western edge of the North American plate, as geologists call the shifting continent, is not always the edge of the continent as delineated on a map, nor does the geologic edge resemble in any way the edge of the earth when all the sailors except Columbus said it was flat. No one will fall off, but being shaken into it is indeed a possibility.

The edge is easy to trace on a geologic map of faults, cracks, and volcanic holes (both dormant and active), its southernmost edge crossing Guatemala from east to west in a dramatic chain of active volcanoes. Guate-

mala City offers some of the most impressive historic earthquake ruins in Central America, and reflecting lakes and volcanic peaks are featured prominently in tourism promotional brochures. Every room in Lago Atitlán resort hotels opens onto grand views of symmetrical volcanic peaks silently fuming from summit craters.

South across the border in the northwest corner of El Salvador is Volcán Izalco, a perfect cone, erupting almost constantly in historic times. The El Salvador government, anticipating considerable tourist business if visitors could view the colorful display from the comfort of a barstool, declared the volcano a national park and constructed a modern hotel complete with cocktail lounge and restaurant on the summit of a nearby mountain viewpoint. Shortly after its completion, I drove up for a drink; it's on a paved scenic highway about an hour's drive west of San Salvador City. All had gone well until the

Pico Orizaba on the great Mexican rift, Mexico.

new Hotel de Montaña opened atop an adjacent mountain, Cerro Verde. As the first excited visitors arrived and drinks were poured, the volcano stopped its show. Volcán Izalco has since been completely silent.

Across Mexico, the "edge" is a hundred-mile-wide region of fire, lava, and ash, spreading northwest astride the highest peaks and lowest valleys, the most notable active volcano being Volcán El Chichón, which erupted with little warning the year after Mt. St. Helens. El Chichón produced a killer ash cloud that burned hundreds of villagers to death, forced thousands more from their homes in surrounding farm communities on the volcano's lower slopes, and created havoc over a wide area. The ash cloud was ejected 18 miles into the stratosphere, where ash was carried around the world on prevailing high-altitude winds. El Chichón's ash cloud eventually covered more than one-quarter of the earth's surface, blocking a significant part of the sun's radiation and producing spectacular sunsets and long romantic twilights in tropical latitudes. All of El Chichón's dust has still not settled.

Nearby Volcán Citlatepetl is a national park and the highest peak in Mexico at 18,701 feet. Only a few miles away is Volcán Orizaba at 18,619 feet, also a national park. Familiar to every tourist arriving by air in Mexico City are the twin snow-capped peaks rising above the city's brown smog, Volcán Popocatepetl and Iztaccihuatl—both national parks, of course. The most expensive homes of wealthy Mexican politicians are built upon thousand-year-old *pahoehoe* lava flows in Mexico City's fancy Pedregal Gardens.

High volcanic peaks and hot holes in the ground continue across Mexico in Del Valle de Santiago, where otherwise flat farmland is pockmarked with small circular craters, from the air looking not unlike a green moonscape. Further west productive corn-

Overleaf: Mules Ear diatreme, southern Utah. Diatremes are associated with volcanic eruptions.

fields of 40 years ago are now a dozen square miles of tumbled black *aa* lava incapable of growing even weeds in the arid climate. Volcán Paricutín now protrudes from the dead landscape, with the white top of a colonial belltower locating the destroyed and buried village of Paricutín.

AT PUERTO VALLARTA is the Pacific, where a great fault rift splits the Gulf of California and continues north for a thousand miles. It's called the San Andreas fault, and it extends many miles into the earth. This sliding, slipping fault edge, actually the eastern edge of the Pacific plate, has been moving inch by inch in a northwesterly direction along the continental plate for millions of years—in any one individual's lifetime no movement at all, yet geological evidence is overwhelming that 15 to 20 million years ago Montara Mountain above Crystal Springs Lakes in the San Andreas fault south of San Francisco was part of the coastal lands of Zihuatanejo and Ixtapa in Mexico.

Beyond Cape Mendocino in northern California, the San Andreas fault turns seaward and, in the area of the largest concentration of earthquakes in coastal North America, meets the eastward-moving Juan de Fuca plate, which is slowly subducting beneath the westward-moving North American continent and in the process keeping Cascade mountain volcanoes active and hot. Off the Oregon shore, undersea volcanoes continue to spew rich deposits of zinc and copper sulfides onto a new crust on the ocean floor.

One Cascades volcano, Mt. St. Helens, erupted in 1980 after 127 years of silence, manifesting its destructive fury on a landscape extending for hundreds of miles, laying flat a forest of thousands of acres, smothering a dozen communities to the northeast with suffocating ash and spreading more into the sky where it continued to circle the earth months later, in the process transforming ordinary late afternoons into glorious sunsets.

Mt. St. Helens in eruption was awesome and at the same time beautiful; frightening and yet peaceful, as ash clouds fell softly to earth in a gray snow. Seen from the interstate highway 30 miles away, the violently billowing ash cloud slowly covered the sky in absolute silence, a slow-motion image of total destruction impossible to comprehend in terms of human-scale events. The violence compares with no other experience.

Over eastern Washington and beyond to Idaho, volcanic ash rich in nutrients fell on wheat and potatoes growing in ancient fields covered with ash 7,000 years ago following the explosive eruption of Mt. Mazama, now Crater Lake, in Oregon. Nature was enriching the earth again, as it has repeatedly over the centuries.

Volcanoes may be gentle, evoking emotional response to the beauty that draws vis-

Columnar basalt, Palisades Rocks, White Pass, Washington.

Layers of ancient ash fallout in John Day Fossil Beds National Monument, eastern Oregon.

itors to the very edge of the erupting firepit, mesmerizing viewers with fountains of lava and surreal flowing rivers of molten rock. A devil's playground is the river of fire, a molten lake, or a privileged glimpse into a crack revealing the earth below, the earth in the beginning.

The sound of an erupting volcano is not gentle; it is the throaty roar of a hundred thunderstorms, creating its own weather front as clouds of heat lower the sky. The heat is a nearby tropical sun at noon; the smells, a sulfurous mix, a witch's brew to match the noise, uncomfortable heat, and unquenchable fire. The most disturbing aspect, even when watching gentle volcanic venting, is the frightening realization that all of this is uncontrollable—we can do nothing except watch the earth churn and boil, understanding that the earth on which we had felt so secure has not yet cooled down, is still an evolving planet in a universe of infinite dimensions, and its final form, if any,

cannot be known. As the earth continues to shake, we can run away, but not far.

The Kodiak seamounts, a scattering of islands below sea level, delineate the edge of the northern continental plate and British Columbia and Alaska, where separate fault rift zones identify earthquake country. At the seaport of Valdez, terminus of the Alaskan oil pipeline and epicenter of the destructive 1964 Alaskan earthquake, waterfront lands sank 30 feet below bay water in minutes after being swept clean by a subsurface-generated tsunami wave. It demonstrated the need for careful consideration of where we live and how we build, as we face somewhat helplessly the major earthquakes and violent volcanic eruptions that will occur at any moment.

THE PHOTOGRAPHS in this book are what our earth looks like—the words are how. How is

Juniper in aa lava flow, Lava Beds National Monument, Tule Lake, California.

the way our shaking earth twists and contorts into the landscapes we place boundaries around and acclaim as unique national parks and monuments, sometimes doing so with difficulty. For a decade before 1980, environmental activists petitioned and lobbied in vain to designate Mt. St. Helens as a national park. Within 12 months after the Cascades volcano erupted in a violent explosion, almost destroying itself, the decimated peak was named Mt. St. Helens National Volcanic Monument.

The movement of the Pacific plate continues to the northwest, as its eastern edge slides against the North American plate. Its movement is inexorable and persistent—the machinery of nature shaping the earth into future forms we can only imagine, shaking our earthly homes in the process, covering cultivated and wild land with smothering volcanic ash, burning the landscape with layers of molten lava. It's as if the earth were starting all over again.

We have built fragile communities on moving faults and on the slopes of active volcanoes, seemingly without regard to impending disaster predicted with qualification by knowledgeable scientists. It has only been in recent years that controversial theories of plate tectonics moved from contemplative academic discussion into assertive statements describing moving continents and hot cracks in the crust as facts. We now accept without much debate early forecasting of earthquakes and eruptions, even tsunami waves as the ocean floor is disturbed by undersea fault movement.

Earthquakes and volcanic activity are an inevitable part of our natural history: the tranquility of a tropical island volcano at rest; the awesome quiet of a vast collapsed volcanic caldera in the New Mexico desert; the first national park in the nation, Yellowstone—the most active geyser basin in the world; San Francisco damming each end of a San Andreas fault valley to make reservoirs for the city's water-supply system; Los Angeles spinning its freeway web into a multimillion-population megatropolis, virtually ignoring the possibility of widespread destruction in a major earthquake—"the big one"—which may occur at any time!

The Los Angeles city government lists several thousand buildings expected to collapse in the predicted quake; homes on unstable clay hillsides will slide into the sea; aqueducts carrying water from northern California will be severed and local distribution systems fractured, drying up water supplies; and as abandoned oil-well shafts snap and rupture underground, trapped methane gas will be released in old neighborhoods and the earth and streets will flame in a conflagration even Hollywood has not dared place on film.

Where our land seems to shake the most and thrust itself violently above surrounding plains and oceans is where we paradox-

McMillan Provincial Park, in the subducting Pacific plate region, Vancouver Island, British Columbia, Canada.

Drowned forest in lake created by an earthquake-induced landslide, Madison River, Montana.

ically like it best, if descriptive words, numerous parks, and great cities are any measure. Californians would never think of leaving home as a consequence of their houses shaking now and then. Neither have residents of Hawaii and of the Pacific Northwest states moved away from mountains that spurt and smoke without warning. Quiet or in eruption, volcanoes are frightening and dangerous, beautiful and awesome, while threatening destruction of everything near, a geological simulation of beauty and the beast.

The earth continues to move, sliding slowly, slipping suddenly, changing in shape and texture even incredibly, as Los Angeles and San Francisco Bay slide closer together and the undersea meeting of immense geologic plates moves toward possible establishment of new continental lands beyond the Pacific Northwest.

It is the dramatic beauty of volcanoes and earthquake country that hides the danger. It is the peace and tranquility of great mountain peaks and tropical islands born of volcanoes that hide frightening episodes of death and destruction we are unable to adequately predict or prevent. We may have inherited the earth, but we have yet to subdue or even control it. We live on the edge of fire.

CHAPTER TWO

Drifting Continents on the Edge of Fire

Volcanic cinder beach, Wailau Valley, Molokai, Hawaii.

It was long ago. Hundreds of millions—perhaps thousands of millions—of years ago, long before the dinosaur and other giant terrestrial carnivorous reptiles became extinct; long before even the smallest of organisms became extant; when life was absent from the land; when a spinning nebula in space became what we call the earth and its newly formed, cooling crust evolved into embryonic continents and oceans drifting forever—the earth as we know it began.

The Pacific, greatest of present-day oceans, its blue expanse covering one-third of the earth's surface, appeared as the new continents drifted into their present location, surrounded by hundreds of active volcanoes—a violent circle of fire and shaking earth. Of the earth's 500-plus volcanoes remaining after the earliest of times and known to have erupted since the beginning of recorded history, 392 lie in a belt encircling the Pacific Ocean—the edge of the continents—and at least 35 more have erupted, such as Hawaii, from the floor of the middle of the vast Pacific area.

The earth as we know it, reported by some who claim to know about these things, apparently began some 4,500 million years ago. The earth that continues shaking in the process of evolving—a planet orbiting through space without apparent limit, spinning over 18,000 miles per hour—is continuing to push and slide earth's land masses effortlessly across a slippery, partially molten interior.

None of us are old enough to have experienced much change in our earth. Few of us have been personally involved in an earthquake or volcanic eruption, a confrontation that frightens us into an intensely knowledgeable understanding of the earth as it flings us through space in transition from a coiling and spinning fiery orb into another yet unknown configuration. An earth without any beginning we know; without, perhaps, any ending at all, or at least nothing we can be certain of. To many of us the earth is

something that began when we first saw it, while we try our best to understand what it is like in our remaining days. We don't see the Grand Canyon getting deeper (yet it is) or see the Big Island of Hawaii sliding to the northwest to sit for awhile in the temporary parking lot now occupied by Maui Island. Our lifespan is just a snap of the fingers compared to the days and years of slow geological change.

PEOPLE LIVING on the western edge of the United States and Mexico live on the edge of fire, part of a Pacific circle of active volcanoes and moving faults completely enclosing the Pacific Ocean rim. Five continents encroach upon the ocean: Asia, Australia, Antarctica, South America, and North America, all of them perpetually drifting about the earth's surface, often disrupting our apparently orderly landscape to create new mountains, change the shape of the seas, and relocate—at times to burn and bury—cities.

With the exception of an occasional contrary boundary and slipping shore, these continents are the plates, as they are called in geophysical terminology. The words and photographs in *The Edge of Fire* describe the western edge of the North American continental plate where it meets the Pacific oceanic plate along the coasts of Central America, Mexico, California, Oregon, Washington, British Columbia, and Alaska. In the east the continental plate extends half way across the Atlantic. Twenty-five million people live on the edge of this shaking and erupting continental plate, subjecting themselves to the erratic whims of a drifting earth that will never settle down and resists attempt to predict its behavior.

The span of geological history is short around most of the Pacific. In Japan, some volcanic and seismic records go back no more

Mango tree in an island forest and erupting east rift vent of Kilauea, Hawaii.

than a thousand years. In Indonesia and the Philippines, modern records did not begin until the arrival of Portuguese, Dutch, and Spanish colonists in the sixteenth century, although legendary accounts tell of volcanic eruptions almost a thousand years ago. For the islands in the middle, written history begins with the British explorer Captain James Cook, sailing Pacific waters at the time of the American Revolution in New England. In more recent times, on the western edge of the North American continent, eight of Father Junipero Serra's adobe missions were shaken to the ground or severely cracked in 1812, but the pioneers who arrived after 1849 were more involved in digging in the earth for precious metals than recording when the earth shook.

It is not known how many volcanic eruptions have gone unrecorded, even in our lifetime, and some may well have been volcanoes with no previously documented eruptive history. In 1910, a light scattering of gray volcanic ash on the leaves of plants and trees in California east of Mt. Shasta indicated that a small eruption possibly occurred in this area. To this day, volcanologists have not discovered precisely which of the dozens of the nearby volcanic cones and buttes may have been the source. Most probably it was a vent on Medicine Lake Volcano near Glass Mountain.

Scattered between and around the historically active volcanoes of the Pacific Rim are many others that, while declared dormant, appear no older. Determining the age of cold volcanoes by measuring the rate of breakdown of radioactive carbon in charcoal buried in their lava flows and volcanic ash, or the decay rate of radioactive potassium to argon, is beginning to give us those dates we missed in the last century. It all is helpful in attempting to predict future volcanic eruptions and earthquakes.

In what is now central Mexico, an entire civilization disappeared about the time of

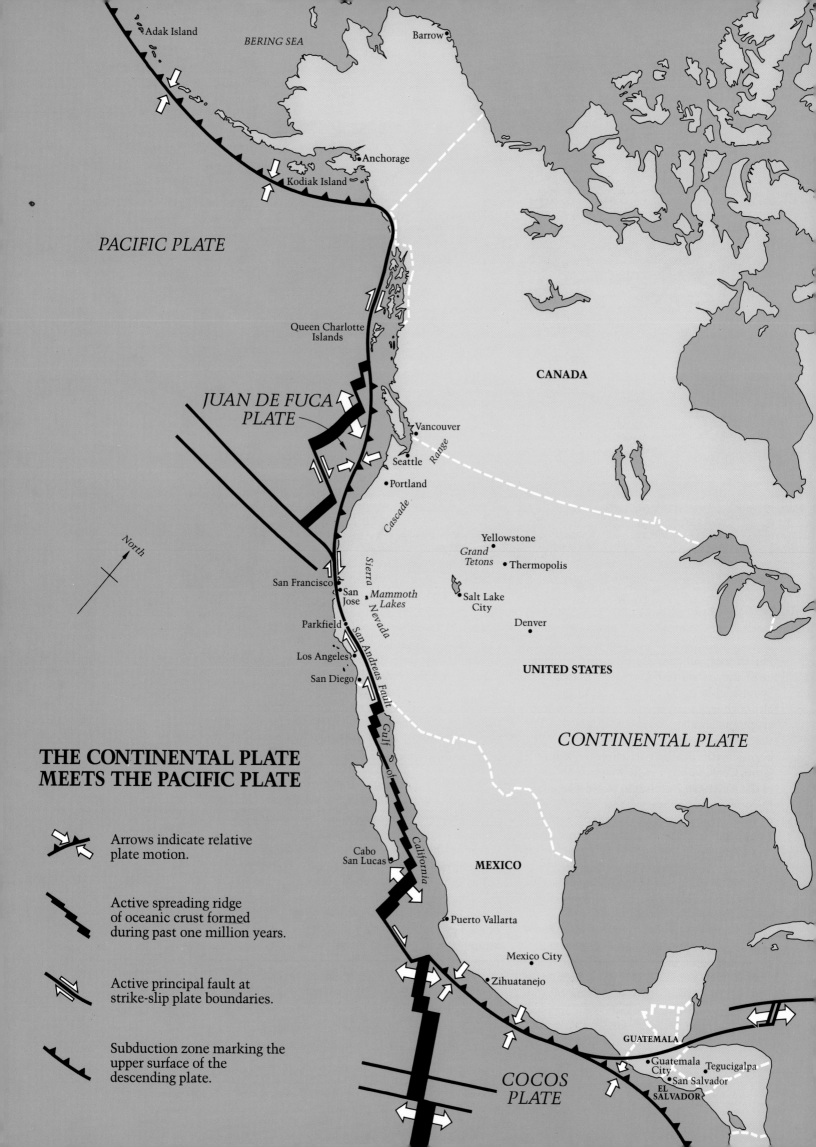

PACIFIC PLATE

BERING SEA

Adak Island

Barrow

Anchorage

Kodiak Island

Queen Charlotte
Islands

*JUAN DE FUCA
PLATE*

CANADA

Vancouver

Seattle

Cascade Range

Portland

Yellowstone

*Grand
Tetons* • Thermopolis

North

San Francisco
San Jose

Parkfield

Los Angeles

San Diego

Sierra Nevada

*Mammoth
Lakes*

Salt Lake
City

Denver

San Andreas Fault

UNITED STATES

CONTINENTAL PLATE

THE CONTINENTAL PLATE
MEETS THE PACIFIC PLATE

Cabo
San Lucas

Gulf of California

MEXICO

Puerto Vallarta

Mexico City

Zihuatanejo

Arrows indicate relative
plate motion.

Active spreading ridge
of oceanic crust formed
during past one million years.

Active principal fault at
strike-slip plate boundaries.

Subduction zone marking the
upper surface of the
descending plate.

GUATEMALA

Guatemala
City Tegucigalpa

EL
SALVADOR San Salvador

*COCOS
PLATE*

Christ when what was then the largest urbanized area in North America, Teotihuacán, was burned and buried in ash fallout from a cataclysmic volcanic eruption. No one recorded the catastrophe.

Our record of volcanic and seismic activity on the Pacific Rim covers less than 200 years. Even today, in many lands around the Pacific Rim, there are few knowledgeable observers; in earlier times even fewer. Not until recent years have eruptions and earthquakes been recorded in any consistent manner, with geologic events compared and consequences evaluated. The science of predicting seismic activity is still in its infancy. As recently as 1946, without any warning, a deadly tsunami, traveling across the ocean at speeds exceeding 350 miles per hour, engulfed the Hawaiian Islands in the central Pacific, smashing into unsuspecting waterfront communities and flooding isolated valleys. In the sea-level settlement of

Laupahoehoe, where an elementary school was located, only one teacher escaped drowning when the school was smashed by the tsunami. Her liferaft was the classroom door.

The 1946 Alaskan tsunami resulted from fault movement on the sea floor in the Aleutian trench, about 90 miles south of Unimak Island. The wave was first seen at Scotch Gap on Unimak when a 115-foot-high wall of water destroyed the Lighthouse. Over 2,000 miles away in Hawaii, several hours later, the wave grew quickly in size as it neared shore, piling up at the entrance to Hilo Bay as a 55-foot-high wall of water. It destroyed nearly 500 oceanside homes and downtown businesses. Property damage amounted to $25 million and more than 150 people died. The wave entered San Francisco Bay about the same time it reached Hawaii, but no one noticed in the bay cities—the wave was only a few inches high inside the Golden Gate.

Columbus Avenue, San Francisco, California, near the edge of the Continental and Pacific plates.

Iztaccihautl and Popocatepetl, volcanoes on the Mexican volcanic rift near Mexico City.

THE AVERAGE DEPTH of the ocean floor below sea level is a little under 3 miles. Continents around the ocean rim rise—in the highest places—to as much as 5 miles above sea level, but continental land masses as a whole average in height only about 1,300 feet above the sea. These two general levels, the continental and the oceanic, relate to fundamental differences in the composition of the earth's crust, which floats and drifts on the mantle heated from within the earth. The continents float higher than the ocean basins because their rocks are lighter, just as a block of cork floats in a bucket of water with its top much higher than that of a similar floating block of oak. Not all of the light continental masses are above sea level, for around its edges the ocean laps over a submerged continental shelf, and in places this true edge of the continent—the foot of the continental plate—lies tens and even hundreds of miles offshore. In some parts of the world large islands are separated from the continent by

shallow seas covering the shelf, seas with a basin resembling the open ocean. Japan is separated from Asia by the oceanic Japan Sea, the Philippines from Asia by the South China Sea, and New Zealand from Australia by the Tasman Sea.

Where near-continent land is the summit of volcanic islands, the volcanoes and their rocks are geologically similar to those found on the edges of the continents. At some future date, they may evolve into larger and larger masses of continental crust that may become welded onto the edge of the continent, may build it outward, or, as in the Pacific Northwest, slide beneath a continent, portions melting again into magma in the process.

Although volcanoes are conspicuous around the rim of the Pacific, most of the coastal mountain ranges are not of volcanic origin. Over millions of years great amounts of sedimentary rock, mostly sandstone and shale, with lesser amounts of limestone and conglomerate, have accumulated along the edges of the continents. These combine with layers of lava and volcanic ash reaching thicknesses as great as 6 miles and more. Forces operating within the earth's crust, extruding magma from the mantle and spreading apart the ocean floor, push both sides of the North American continent closer together. As geologic forces continue, in places the deformation becomes so great that the rocks break and one side of the split slides past the other. As a result of folding and faulting, masses of sedimentary rock are pushed into ridges, many of which rise above the sea to form lines of islands, much like those offshore of southern California. Others have moved ashore and become welded to the edges of the continents to form coastal mountain ranges. Further inland, massive upthrusts of the crust along faulting weak sections of the earth produce higher mountains. The Sierra Nevada and Grand Tetons, for example, are gigantic mountains being forced upward in a continuing squeeze. These

complex movements of the earth's crust, far beneath the oceans and across the continents, are secondary effects of the movement of continental plates.

Forces involved in this drifting of the continents atop the mantle are sometimes compared to the thermal convection seen in a kettle of thick soup cooking on the stove; the liquid at the bottom expands and rises to the top in a continuous circular movement. Consider the mantle on which the crust moves as hot "silly putty" that changes shape when subjected to steady, if quite gentle, forces. The convection flow, perhaps given impetus by radioactive heating and churning deeper within the earth, provides the driving mechanism for continental drift, the spreading of oceans, and the crumpling of flat landscapes into mountains.

The speed of this convection flow carrying the continents is estimated to be no more than a fraction of an inch per year. It would take about 200 million years for fresh magma

Ship Rock, ancient volcanic core, New Mexico.

Exposed extruded magma in ancient vent crack, Church Rock, Kayenta, Arizona.

from Pacific Ocean rifts to move toward the North American continent and slide beneath it to rejoin the molten mantle. This action would produce earthquakes and volcanoes in the process of constantly renewing the ocean floor. Because the continents are composed of much lighter material they cannot sink into the mantle; they stay on top and drift, responding gently to convection currents beneath.

Deep inside the core of sedimentary rock, pressure and high temperatures have altered the rocks into new types: sandstones became quartzites, limestones became marbles, and shales and impure clay sandstones were changed to mica-bearing schists. Still greater changes altered some schists to gneisses, while some gneisses melted to form massive granite. Some magma may work its way

upward into the upper crust where it eventually cools and crystallizes to form great granitic masses known as plutons, such as Half Dome in Yosemite. Other magma, finding its way to the surface along faults, erupts as volcanoes.

No sooner do upthrusting mountain ridges raise their tops above surrounding flat country than they are attacked by erosion. During the Ice Age it was glaciers; since then stormy seas saw away at mountain edges; rain falling on slopes cuts gullies and then canyons. Exposure to weather breaks down rocks into soil, which moves steadily downslope into streams and then into rivers, and masses of earth on the gouged steep slopes break loose as landslides by this great leveling process. All of these processes together carve the ridges into valleys, hills, and mountains. Given time

San Andreas Fault (bottom of image), Temblor Range, southern California.

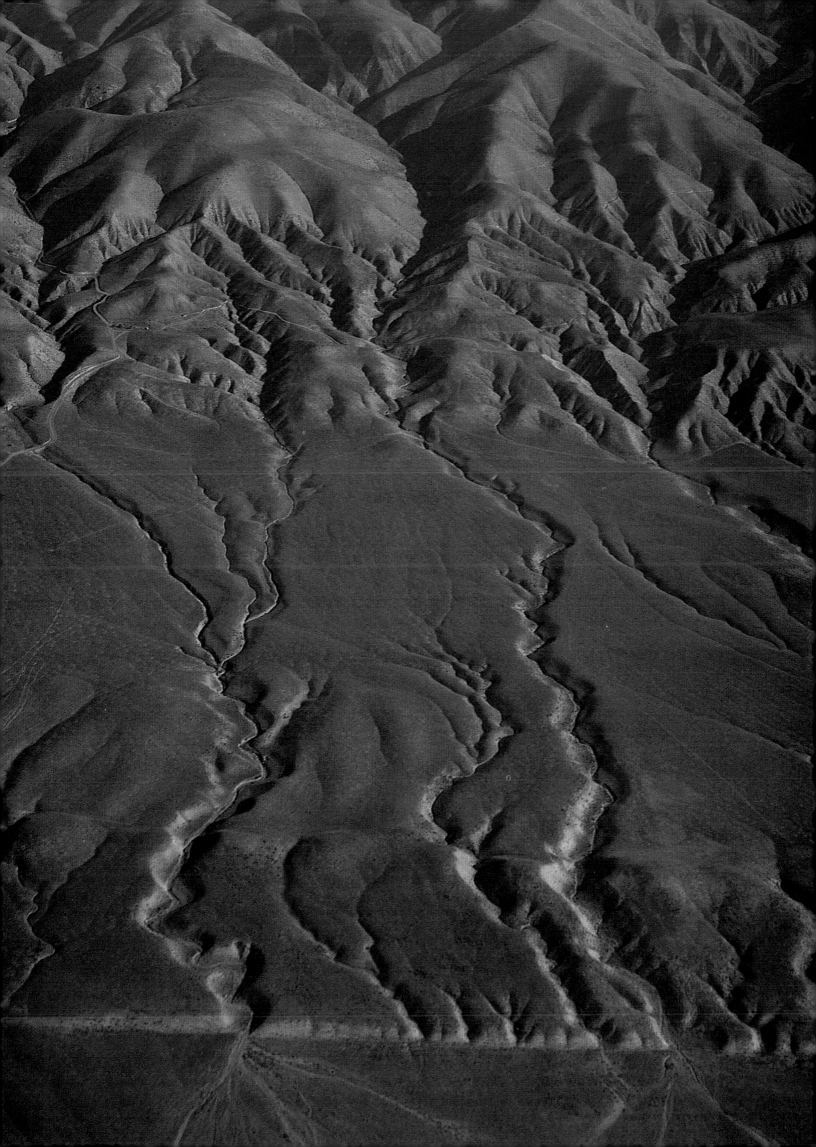

Puu O Maui cinder cone, Haleakala Crater, Haleakala National Park, Hawaii.

the rising ridges are cut by great rivers into deep canyons as the continents rise higher above the mantle and the rivers cut into the earth on their way to the sea. This is clearly seen in places such as the Grand Canyon of the Colorado and the Columbia River Gorge.

Most earthquakes—and all the big ones— are the result of fault slippage as rocks on one side of a fault move past those on the other side. This grating movement causes the vibrations we call earthquakes. It is simply a trembling of the ground, a shimmying of the rocks of the earth and the buildings we have built there. Faults do not move freely, and the rocks on one side are bent and held in a highly stressed condition; the accumulating strain increases until it overcomes irregularities in the rock holding everything in place. Suddenly the rocks are forced past each other, sliding to a stop where friction prevents further movement. This elastic rebound releases a large amount of energy

stored in the bent rocks, and it appears to be the cause of all very violent earthquakes, some so violent they can set the entire state of California resonating in aftershocks. The role of faults in generating earthquakes was first recognized during studies of the San Andreas fault following the 1906 San Francisco earthquake and fire, when obvious deformation of roads and fence lines could be accounted for in no other way.

It is this sudden movement of faults— where blocks of the earth slide horizontally past each other and move vertically in areas of upthrust pressures—that causes most earthquakes along the Pacific Rim. Extensive areas of western states, particularly California, are a maze of breaks, splits, and cracks identifying stresses placed upon the straining surface crust of the continent as it bulges and stretches. It is no coincidence that the continental edge produces the swarms of earthquakes for which California is famous.

Mountain building and crustal crumpling movements along the edge have resulted in some of the most disastrous earthquakes in history—the destructive 1906 San Francisco quake, the Tokyo earthquake of 1923, and the Hawk's Bay earthquake of 1931 in New Zealand.

Other quakes are caused by movement of magma near the earth's surface. Molten rock enters old volcanic cracks and under tremendous pressure is forced upward, pushing apart ancient cracks and causing the surface ground to actually bulge outward and vibrate in the process. Earthquakes on the eastern Sierra Nevada escarpment near Mono Lake are likely the result of magma approaching to within perhaps 4 miles below the surface of a 600-year-old volcanic caldera now filled with the condominiums and shopping centers of Mammoth Lakes Resort. Frequent earthquakes are felt throughout the area and, just in case the lava plume escapes to the surface, local authorities have constructed an emergency escape road for residents when the main entrance road to the community is broken.

Still another cause of earthquakes in coastal regions is the sudden movement of a deep oceanic plate sliding beneath the continental plate, a shift of the ocean floor that was undoubtedly the cause of the destructive 1985 Mexico City earthquake. The moving Cocos plate offshore of Acapulco slid beneath the relatively fixed continental plate.

IN TERMS OF SIZE, we generally think of an earthquake as big or small, but this definition depends, of course, on how far away we are from the epicenter—the place where the fault or the pushing magma shifts in a sudden jump, slips in a long slide, or merely cracks the earth a little. At times the fault just creeps along quietly and nobody notices anything.

Land's End at Cabo San Lucas, Baja California Sur.

Earthquake magnitudes are generally measured using a scale devised by Charles Richter. In his scale, when the severity of shaking increases by one unit, the shaking amplitude has increased ten times. The infamous San Francisco quake of 1906 was an estimated 8.25 on the Richter scale, which was 30 times more severe than the 1971 southern California earthquake in the San Fernando Valley, a 7.5 shake. Mexico City's destructive 1985 quake, with an epicenter many hundreds of miles away in the Pacific Ocean west of Acapulco, caused the collapse of many high buildings and measured 8.1 on the Richter scale. The energy released by a Richter-scale 8 earthquake approximates the explosive force of 10,000 atomic bombs of the size dropped on Hiroshima. No scientists were around to measure the 1868 Kau earthquakes on the Big Island of Hawaii. The swarm of Kau quakes lasted five days and shook to the ground every structure in the area. Even animals and people couldn't stand on their feet.

The Pacific Ring of Fire, its earthquakes and volcanoes, is part of an active geologic zone of mountain building, with folding and breaking of rocks on the surface, lateral shifting of the earth's crust in extensive faults deep within the earth, and subduction of oceanic tectonic plates beneath the continents. All create active volcanoes and a landscape that is constantly changing into new forms, often moving to new locations in the process.

The most famous moving piece of continent, easily seen by astronauts from outer space, is the sliver of coastal land west of the San Andreas fault, which extends from the tip of Cabo San Lucas in Mexico northwest to where the fault enters the ocean again a hundred miles north of San Francisco. This gigantic section of the continent has been slipping northwest for at least 30 million years, beginning long before the drifting continents were arbitrarily fixed in their present location by global mapmakers who decided the continents never moved and that cartographers could safely draw the coastal edge without having to erase their inked lines.

The continents are drifting on a sea of putty-like rafts heated in an oven of radioactive decay on a plastic lithospheric ocean. The shapes are recognized only in cartographic projections of global contours assumed to be permanent—but they were not and are not. In terms of geologic time, an accurate view of the earth is difficult for us to assimilate. We have always assumed that everything has always been this way. The millions of years of earth history are impossible to comprehend. (The Bible uses days.) Yet the earth continues to evolve and its Pacific Ring of Fire—with volcanoes manifesting beauty and destruction—and its other geological phenomena are constant reminders of continuing mountain building and faulting. Earthquakes daily reveal new fundamental relationships in the movement of crustal plates, in the spreading ocean floors, and in the invincible drifting continents, the only place we have for living on earth.

Lava flow beneath ocean surface, La Parouse Bay, Maui, Hawaii.

CHAPTER THREE

Suffocating a Civilization

Pyramid of the Moon, Cerro Gordo, Teotihuacán, Mexico.

The Managua International Airport in Nicaragua was a shambles when I arrived from Miami. Except for the airline ticket counters, very little had been repaired following the 1972 earthquake that killed perhaps 10,000 people in Managua City. It was not a building I would consider safe in another quake. Jagged cracks exposed gray concrete in supporting columns, and rusty reinforcing steel and peeling paint revealed shattered masonry walls already changing back to sand. I was pleased to be only a transiting passenger and looked in anticipation at the Pan American 707 waiting for me on the ramp outside the terminal. In the air I would feel considerably more secure than in the terminal on the ground in shaky Nicaragua. I was reminded of the decision by French canal builders who were seriously considering a canal route across Nicaragua until they saw local postage stamps depicting an active volcano. They decided Panama would be a better location.

After landing in El Salvador, I was en route by cab to the Westin Camino Real Hotel in San Salvador City when I realized a mistake had been made—I had flown to the wrong country! I wanted to be in Guatemala, the next country to the north.

My plans were to photograph the great Guatemalan volcanoes along the southern edge of the North American continental plate, and it was during this inadvertent stopover in El Salvador that I learned of archaeological excavations in volcanic ash around Lago de Ilopango, an ancient collapsed caldera near San Salvador not unlike Crater Lake in Oregon. These were the Mayan highlands, a densely populated agricultural community about 1,700 years ago, before a destructive series of major volcanic eruptions occurred in the vicinity of Ilopango caldera, some possibly erupting through the lake waters, intensifying the ash clouds that spread over thousands of square miles.

The ash fallout resulted from explosive eruptions in which molten rock containing dissolved gas rose quickly in the volcano's vent, suddenly separating into lava and bubbles. The bubbles expanded rapidly in the air, burst the surrounding lava, and separated into a mixture of fine particles and gas driven together from the volcano by the force of its own expansion. The resulting material was hurled far above the volcano vent where it cooled into a fine ash and was caught and blown many hundreds of miles away, falling to earth at times in places where no one was aware a volcano was actually erupting.

The gray ash slowly fell from the sky, silently covering productive farmlands and population centers in what is now El Salvador and parts of Guatemala. The smothering ash fallout was many feet thick in places and effectively halted the growth of Mayan civilization in the highlands. It was a disaster for the Mayas comparable to the violent and sudden volcanic eruption on the Greek island of Thera in the fifteenth century B.C., precipitating the destruction of Minoan civilization. It must have been many decades before partial recovery of vegetation and wildlife populations allowed the descendants of the highland Mayas to return. For most, it was more practical to move onto untouched lands farther north, where their slash-and-burn agriculture began new cycles in the tropical forest.

Destruction of the highland ecology, with the land rendered uninhabitable by Volcán Ilopango, quite certainly forced a major migration to northeastern Guatemala, precipitating rapid Mayan expansion and building at Tikal and other sites in the Petén jungle. Thousands of refugees escaped death from hot ash clouds but were unable to farm the desiccated landscape. This forced rapid urbanization of the primarily religious centers, accelerated cultural development, and became an important catalyst in the flowering of Mayan civilization in the Petén. Major north-south trade routes were soon established between population centers in the Yucatan and central Mexico.

Tikal and surrounding settlements, located at an apparently safe distance from volcanoes to the southwest, were soon ringed by a sophisticated network of drainage canals, which transformed swamps from uncultivatible wasteland into highly productive agricultural lands that fed thousands of residents. Tikal became perhaps the first true city of the New World, an extensive concentration of public architecture, temple pyramids, and art, the bounty of an advanced civilization unlike any other in Mesoamerica. Its very complexity, supporting a religious bureaucracy and depending upon the easily disrupted fragile canal network required for agriculture in the swamps, may have made inevitable an end to Mayan civilization in a land of destructive earthquakes and active

volcanoes. It was only a matter of time before friction deep within the earth between shifting continental plates would produce another cataclysmic event along the Guatemalan rift.

CRYSTAL-BLUE LAGO ATITLÁN in central Guatemala floods a large valley, an explosion-created caldera, rimmed by three active volcanoes—Tolimán, Atitlán, and San Pedro—while other high volcanic peaks hover behind Guatemala City and along the great rift running the length of the country. Few Guatemalan cities have remained in their original location very long. Among the casualties was the second capital built by Spanish conquerors, established in Almolonga Valley in 1527 and destroyed 14 years later in 1541 after torrential rains filled the inactive crater of Volcán Agua and an earthquake cracked it open, flooding the town. Survivors established a

Amatitlan Volcano, Guatemala.

new city nearby, now known as Antigua Guatemala, which remained the capital despite numerous punishing quakes until the destructive 1773 Santa Maria earthquake created its havoc. Then the politicians moved out and built a new capital they called Guatemala City, locating it 40 miles east on a high plateau known as La Ermita, Valley of the Virgin. Like its predecessor, the capital was repeatedly wracked by tremors until 1917 and 1918, when it was virtually leveled, but no other suitable site was found for relocation, and the city was rebuilt on the ruins of the old.

Standing atop the highest Tikal temple, the visitor sees a flat, green landscape extending forever into the distant horizon without the interruption of fuming volcanic peaks. Only the highest temple structures atop towering pyramids are seen above the humid jungle canopy. The Mayas must have felt quite secure in their homes surrounding the Tikal temples, far from the ominous rumblings of the Atitlán volcano to the southwest and volcanic venting in the northwestern valley of Mexico.

Their confidence was misplaced. Climbing atop the Tikal structures still unexcavated by archaeologists digging into the Mayan past, I kicked the toe of my boot into light grey ash, the same dusty volcanic ash I had found in the coffee plantations around Atitlán—the same ash that is the soil of the rich farmlands in El Salvador and the dust covering Honduras. In the Tikal ruins my fingers dug into clay-like ash covered by twisting roots of tropical trees wrapped around ancient stone, reaching into ragged cracks to split the temples apart before archaeologists could nudge out their lost secrets. The reason for abandonment of these great temples was no longer a mystery. The answer was everywhere in Tikal and for hundreds of miles in all directions. It was not mysterious why the Mayas hurriedly left their cities and fled north to the apparent safety of the Yucatan peninsula. It was not possible to grow food crops and live in a suffocating sea of volcanic ash. They fled death. The Aztecs later wrote in the *Codex Telleriano*, "The era will end when earthquakes swallow all things and the stars are shaken down from the sky."

The people called Olmec, living in lowland swamps along the eastern coast of the Gulf of Mexico, perhaps emerged from the Mayas migrating northward and were part of a once continuous strip of Mayan-speaking people extending from somewhat south of Guatemala into the Yucatan peninsula and farther to the northern shore of the Gulf of Mexico. Aztec legends describe a place called Tamoanchan, which in Aztec Nahuatl makes no sense but in Mayan refers to a "Land of the Rainy Sky," an apt description of swamp country on the Gulf.

Reflecting religious attitudes of two thousand years ago, the Mayas, Olmecs, and Aztecs thought of rain from the sky not just as water but also as a rain of "celestial fire"— hot lava and volcanic ash. Continuous volcanic activity, lighting the night sky in a perpetual sunset, was geologic reality in preconquest Mesoamerica—as spiritually awesome as the sun and stars, as much a part of life as day and night.

La Venta in Tabasco, perhaps the greatest of Olmec city-temple sites, was located on a two-square-mile island at sea level about 18 miles inland from the Gulf. Rising from the flat island, now desecrated by oil-company bulldozers, air strips, and parking lots, is a major Olmec ceremonial pyramid, the largest of its period in Mexico. Unlike all the others, La Venta pyramid has the shape of a volcano, with fluted side slopes and an unmistakable crater at its peak. It is almost as if the Olmecs created their own volcano to appease destructive gods, raising the temple into the sky as if to intercept the rain.

Flourishing as traders and craftsmen, the Olmecs have been described by an eminent Mexican scholar as the "first and finest sculptors of Mexico." They carved small jade objects by the thousands, apparently preferring to work in the hardest jade, including an apple-green jade mined in eastern Guatemala. The Olmecs were also artists in stone. Colossal heads up to ten feet in height and weighing many tons were chiseled with typical Olmec fat lips and scowls from volcanic basalt, a rock not found in the La Venta–San Lorenzo Olmec region but 50 miles or more away on the slopes of volcanic Cintepec in the Tuxtla Mountains. Here the raw volcanic material was quarried from selected boulders and then dragged to shallow streams, loaded on rafts, and floated along the coast and upriver to religious sites. Carved without benefit of metal tools and transported

Olmec tomb of columnar basalt, Villahermosa, Mexico.

miles by land and sea without wheeled transport, the magnificent and awe-inspiring Olmec basalt sculptures are testimony to an advanced civilization benefiting from crosscultural fertilization as they were forced from stagnating cities by "celestial rains" emanating from the most active rift of volcanoes in Central America.

La Venta and San Lorenzo evidently were destroyed deliberately by their own inhabitants. Most of the sculptured monuments were intentionally mutilated, and the temples and surrounding irrigated farmland abandoned to the jungle. The Olmec lands are covered with the same gray ash found elsewhere in Mesoamerica—volcanic ash that created soft earthen mounds over community structures and, in one Olmec locality, completely buried a tomb constructed of columnar basaltic logs. Could it be that temples, built to placate the gods of fire spewing

from beneath the earth and fire raining from the skies, had failed the ancient priests, causing them to destroy images of an ineffectual religion?

For whatever reason, the downfall of Olmec La Venta may have inspired the even greater classic city-state of Teotihuacan, where a magnificent ceremonial avenue, over two miles long and faced by two of the largest pyramids outside of Egypt, was constructed in a valley enclosed by 65 active volcanic peaks and cinder vents. The torch of Mesoamerican civilization was passed to a new site surrounded by volcanoes, as if to directly challenge the powerful rain god Tlaloc in his home. The Olmec and Mayan tradition of temple building and city planning reached new heights at Teotihuacán, where a great metropolis was built—the largest city in the Americas at the time, covering almost seven square miles. Teotihua-

Above: Detail of La Venta Olmec head carved from basalt, Villahermosa, Mexico.

Below: La Venta Olmec head, from San Lorenzo, Mexico. Carved from basalt, the head stands 10 feet high and weighs 20 tons.

cán would eventually house a population of perhaps 200,000, until it, too, was in turn destroyed and buried.

Teotihuacán didn't just grow by chance at the site of a trading crossroads. The city was carefully planned as an important metropolis and religious center, with a great ceremonial avenue, public squares, and elaborate pyramids. Transient housing, craftwork shops, quarters for priests, and, by one count, over 2,000 apartment compounds were constructed on geometric grid blocks. Buildings and pyramids were often renewed as generations passed, with new structures built on top of the old without disturbing original temples and public areas.

The city was built on the gentle slope of an ancient lava flow emanating from Volcán Tecomaxuchitl. Beyond the lava, a complex network of irrigated fields produced premium agricultural crops in a variety found nowhere else in the world. Buildings were constructed mostly of materials quarried from the site, as were weapons and domestic ceramics. Skilled artisans in hundreds of shops made jewelry and ornaments from black volcanic obsidian as well as from imported green and ivory jade. The metropolis was self-sustaining to a remarkable degree and also a great center of commerce, the well-chosen site being astride important trade routes leading south to Mexico and Guatemala and west and east to the Pacific Ocean and the Gulf of California.

Archaeologist Michael Coe noted in a 1971 report, "The importance of volcanic obsidian for the economy of ancient Mesoamerican peoples was probably similar in magnitude to that of steel for the economies of modern industrial nations." Most of their weapons—knives and arrowheads—were made from obsidian. The tools used were of obsidian. Rene Millon of the University of Rochester identified during his excavations more than 500 craft-workshop sites in the city environs, most of them used for working in obsidian. A rich source of the black volcanic "glass" lay nearby in a sheet formed between layers of red ash and lava during a prior eruption on the northeastern edge of the valley. The Teotihuacános no doubt considered obsidian—whose blades never lose their sharp edge—a necessity for existence and its abundance a logical reason to estab-

lish their city amidst the feared yet valuable volcanoes.

The city of Teotihuacán was built on a grandiose scale. Destined to be the largest urban center on the American continent, it was larger than the walled city of Imperial Rome and was a religious and cultural center, a political and economic capital. The immense city was the largest preindustrial city in the world and the seat of a popular religion with undoubtedly widespread support, headed conceivably by a pontiff in a city attracting pilgrims from afar, as do contemporary Benares and Mecca. The population supported a teeming marketplace and attracted thousands to its scheduled market days for trade and a wide variety of agricultural products.

At a time when medieval Europe was suffering from malnutrition and a monotonous and dreary diet (before spices from the Orient arrived to disguise spoiled meat), the citizens of Teotihuacán enjoyed abundant foodstuffs that would not be tasted by Europeans for another 400 years. The Teotihuacán market displayed chocolate (in the form of cocoa beans), maize, pumpkins and squash, potatoes, tomatoes, numerous kinds of beans, a hundred varieties of pepper, pineapple, strawberries, persimmons, peanuts, avocados, guinea pigs and turkeys, even cocaine. Being able to offer such a variety of fresh produce and animals in the market was the rewarding outcome of years of agricultural development by an extremely knowledgeable people, a civilization in the New World comparable with any in the Old World of European serfs and knights.

The people of Teotihuacán always associated their destiny with Cerro Gordo ("Fat Mountain"), the volcanic peak rising directly behind the Pyramid of the Moon, a volcano that probably was mostly quiet during the years when Teotihuacán flourished. Cerro Gordo was the source of the city's water, with some 80 springs, it is reported, all of them concentrated on the "fat" mountain's lower slopes; the water was contained within a giant internal reservoir sealed by impervious lava dikes extruded under pressure into the mountain. As the major source of Teotihuacán's agricultural wealth, Cerro Gordo surely accounted for the obvious orientation of the entire city plan and the monumental Ave-

Cerro Tlaloc, Valley of Mexico, near Mexico City.

nue of the Dead, all directly aligned with the volcano.

In later years, the Aztecs would tell of Tlaloc, a god of rain from the sky—water, lava, or ash. Every mountain where rain clouds gathered was Tlaloc. The Aztecs later related how "time ended when volcanic eruptions occurred and fire and cinders rained down out of the sky to consume the earth" and how in the general immolation the people became birds in order to survive the catastrophe.

Every guidebook, every history I have read about Teotihuacán attempts to explain the demise of the great Teotihuacáno city by invoking legendary "barbarians from the north" who sacked, burned, and buried the city. Apart from questioning the repeated assertion that barbarians always came from the north, I was unable to accept the claim that Teotihuacán was actually burned and

buried by anyone. The urban complex was simply too extensive, too many square miles for what would have had to be a simple act of revenge against a peaceful population. It didn't make sense.

The Spanish conquistadores destroyed the Aztec capital of Tenochtitlan but did not bury the city. They built a new city atop the old— Mexico City. The largest structure in the world at the time was the Aztec pyramid at Cholula where the Spanish solution to the religious problem was to level off the top of the pyramid, bring in some landscaping, and build their own Catholic church there. They were completely unaware that this is precisely what the Aztecs and previous ruling peoples had already done several times before—built a new pyramid atop the old. The priests at Teotihuacán had done the same in rebuilding the Temple of Quetzalcoatl. There was no need to destroy the city.

I stood on the top platform of the Pyramid of the Moon and looked directly at the summit of Volcán Cerro Gordo, trying to understand the city's fate and visualize what had happened. I looked around at the dozens of volcanic cones enclosing the valley. As I had in El Salvador and again atop Tikal in Guatemala, I kicked the toe of my boot into gray ash still covering the unexcavated rear portion of the pyramid. At the base of the nearby Pyramid of the Sun, almost a mile down the ceremonial avenue, I strained more of the same ash through my fingers as I dug into the ground. Roofless apartments near the base of the pyramid were buried in volcanic ash to what had been the roof eaves. Their interior rooms, now excavated, look like basements. I could almost see the desolate, moonlike landscape first seen by the Aztecs when they ventured into Teotihuacán Valley looking for a lost civilization.

Early archaeologists soon discovered that, as quickly as they uncovered a structure, the exposed wall would be rapidly eroded by rain and by weeds sprouting in the clay mortar used by the original Teotihuacán builders. (Workers restoring the city replaced clay with cement mortar studded with lava rock fragments.) Colorful murals that had been protected over the years by the ash quickly blown against their surface during the eruption faded rapidly when exposed to the humid Mexican climate. It was, to me, proof of yet another volcanic catastrophe in the history of Mesoamerica.

The dead city had lain silent for hundreds of years before inquisitive Aztecs dug into the ruins, followed by European archaeologists after the Spanish conquest. In 1884, Leopoldo Batres, the first native Mexican to do extensive excavations, reported that wherever he dug "there was evidence of a great fire," which had destroyed buildings "like a terrible Troy." Batres found that "the upper

Cerro Gordo, Teotihuacán, Mexico.

parts of walls where they joined the flat roofs were charred, and many rafters had fallen to the floor, where they lay carbonized."

Inside excavated apartments he found skeletons of men, women, and children lying about in different positions, not having been able to escape the fiery holocaust that descended upon them. Skeletons still wore necklaces of small stones that had not melted from the heat. According to Batres, it was hard for him to believe "that anything but an earthquake followed by fire could have so thoroughly destroyed a city." Charred areas around most of the pyramids and public buildings attested to the fury of the catastrophe that destroyed Teotihuacán. The city and surrounding farmlands, when Batres first saw them, were completely covered with gray ash. The dwellings and pyramids had been transformed into smooth mounds and embankments, the streets into valleys where indigenous plants and trees flourished on the arid landscape. The once great city had become shrouded in an earthen blanket that hid the metropolis for a thousand years.

The end of Teotihuacán may have occurred with little warning. Perhaps it was noted, without concern, that a lava fountain erupting from the volcanic summit was higher than usual, when suddenly an incandescent cloud of ash and pumice exploded from the mountain, traveling downhill with increasing turbulence at incredible speed toward the unsuspecting city—a glowing windstorm of fire with temperatures probably exceeding 2000° Fahrenheit. Teotihuacán was set afire and buried, probably within hours.

It had been predicted long before, when the god Nanahuatl sacrificed himself to become the present sun, that the final end would occur "when the earth has become tired, when already it is so, when the seed of the earth has ended." Many other volcanoes in central Mexico also erupted during this period. The immense lava flow called Pedregal on the southern edge of Mexico City poured forth during these times. Teotihuacán was the American Pompeii.

Forest trees were stripped of their leaves, large branches broken, and saplings bent to the ground and covered with ash. Crops were smothered and agriculture was rendered impossible. Where maize had been planted, germinating seedlings met with a harsh environment that allowed only stunted plants

to survive. As ash continued to fall following the initial eruption, undernourished seedlings were stripped of new leaves or covered by ash falling faster than maize could grow, while fungus diseases penetrated bruised plants and inhibited growth. Teotihuacán farmers who returned hoping to reestablish their fields found solid volcanic ash unsuitable for planting, and as they struggled with wooden plows that were unable to penetrate to the original soil below, they watched their seedlings die.

Fruit trees were defoliated by falling ash, and fine dust-like ash blew into avocado flowers, preventing pollination. Ashfalls killed honey bees, birds, and flies, adversely affecting ecological relationships between insects and plants. Harmful fruit flies were eliminated, but the ashfall also killed other beneficial insects. Larger animals were smothered in the first hot ash fallout by the fluorine, chlorine, and sulfur compounds and carbon dioxide released by the ash. Sheep throughout the countryside died from fluorine poisoning when they ate contaminated grass.

Water-transported ash choked streams and destroyed irrigation systems, killing fish and food for the wildlife that had not yet suffocated from breathing volcanic ash. Following decimation of the forest there was a gradual decline in rainfall, changing the valley from a place of tropical showers to a semiarid desert. Deforestation resulted in destructive erosion and lowering of the water table. Streams silted up with ash. Seeps and springs dried up. By now, foodstuffs and buyers had long ago disappeared from the great marketplace, and merchants no longer traveled the trade routes with crafts of obsidian and jade. Priests became refugees. Not only had the social and cultural relationships been destroyed but political and economic life as well. Teotihuacán ceased to exist.

Before the final volcanic eruption—and there have been none since the city was destroyed—the valley surrounding the great city of Teotihuacán was undoubtedly a vast tropical forest filled with abundant game. Adjoining cultivated fields, streams, and lakes offered shelter and food for fish and aquatic birds. Ample water was available for irrigated crops. Urban cultural life thrived in a civilization advanced for its time, until human ecological relationships with the land

Statue of Tlaloc, one of the oldest and most prevalent of Mesoamerican gods, Museo Nacional de Antropologia, Mexico City.

were totally destroyed over perhaps a thousand square miles. No creature, not even the insect population, was spared. Even if exiled residents had wanted to rebuild, they would have found it difficult to survive there. Paradise had temporarily become a sterile desert. It would not have been unlike a nuclear winter.

Refugees fleeing sudden death in their city would have probably settled to the south in Azcapotzalco and near Lake Texcoco, where the Aztec civilization would eventually flourish. Like the Aztecs, Teotihuacános did not accept the concept of eternity and eternal repetitiveness.

They made no attempt to rebuild their city.

SEEDS WILL EVENTUALLY blow into devastated areas, or be carried in by birds—in time, colonization will begin. Life soon begins its inexorable comeback, if only by elemental organisms that thrive on the chemical compounds dissolved in the boiling water and stream. The ash itself may offer a rich source of nutrition and minerals for many plants. Within a year after the explosion of Mt. St. Helens, some plants and animals were already returning, but most will find survival difficult. People will find Mt. St. Helens suitable for only short visits for many decades to come.

The cataclysmic explosion of Mt. Mazama in Oregon, creating present day Crater Lake, threw light weight pumice and other mineral crystals and rock fragments several miles above the collapsing volcano, from where northeasterly winds blew the ash over thousands of square miles, extending as far as 800 miles distant. On the lower slopes of the erupting mountain, the ash fallout was ten feet thick, while in British Columbia and Montana, perhaps only a gentle dusting occurred. It may well be that the excellent-draining soil making for bountiful potato crops in Idaho today is the consequence of ash fallout from Mt. Mazama some 6,600 years ago.

Unlike the ecologically destructive Cerro Gordo eruption at Teotihuacán, the eruption of smaller Sunset Crater in northern Arizona about 900 years ago, spreading ash and cinder over 800 square miles, enabled early Indians to build permanent communities and grow crops in the Wupatki area while the

Pyramid of the Sun, Teotihuacán, Mexico.

eruption was still going on. Some archaeologists believe a virtual "land rush" was started when the ash, acting as a moisture-retaining mulch, made possible intensive agriculture on the previously semi-desert, arid lands.

Continuing study of volcanic ash fallout, which in the past has been little considered in evaluating archaeological excavations, may give us a clearer understanding of historical events and migrations of indigenous people. Ash falls cannot be prevented, but increased

Temple of Quetzalcoatl, Teotihuacán, Mexico.

Lava flow in Pedregal Garden district, Mexico City.

knowledge of their characteristics can help the public understand possible adverse consequences and prevent chaos. It is good to know what event overtook the Mayas and Teotihuacános, the people of Crete and Pompeii, the Pacific Northwest, and the Indians at Wupatki.

EIGHT HUNDRED YEARS after Teotihuacanos fled their city, in 1985, the subducting oceanic plate, still sliding beneath the continent deep in the ocean off Mexico, vibrated the ocean floor sufficiently to cause an eight-inch tsunami wave at Hilo Bay, Hawaii.

Before the mini-tsunami had reached the islands over 2,500 miles distant, Mexico City, a shorter 235 miles inland, was hit by a 7.8 quake killing an estimated 7,000 residents,

leaving 150,000 homeless, and presenting an earthquake bill to the Mexican government of at least $4 billion. Major high rise office buildings collapsed, 450 schools broke apart, nine hospitals were damaged beyond repair, and $186 million worth of hotel rooms were destroyed. The soft, dry lake bed on which Mexico City is built amplified the seismic shocks into an unprecedented fury. The city was not destroyed—most of the 18 million population survived—but the government and politicians were suddenly exposed to unexpected scrutiny from which they may never recover.

Earthquakes are often described as acts of God, and in Central America the disturbing phenomenon have frequently triggered major changes in the local political establishment. Autocratic juntas have been violently shaken on more than one occasion from their otherwise secure seats of power. In 1810, during Venezuela's war of independence, an earthquake suddenly battered colonial Caracas. It was taken as a sign by these early freedom fighters that even the forces of nature, as well as God, were on the side of revolution and against Spanish colonialism.

After a major earthquake destroyed most of Nicaragua's capital city in 1972, Dictator Anastasio Somoza initiated a $6 billion reconstruction program to rebuild Managua, where almost every business and industry had been seriously damaged. Over the next seven years, while the city languished in weeds and ruin, it became apparent that the Somoza family were enriching themselves personally, diverting financial resources sent from abroad into their Miami bank account. The abuse of power turned even the middle classes against Somoza, precipitating a successful seizure of power by the Sandinistas.

Guatemala City suffered an earthquake more severe than Mexico City in 1976, when over 22,000 were killed, 74,000 injured, and 340,000 made homeless. The military rulers at the time did little to help. Priests, nuns and lay Catholic workers organized self-help groups in working class neighborhoods and mobilized the poor to pressure the government and demand assistance. Soon after the quake, guerrilla forces also began recruiting in Guatemala City and in a short time grew into a formidable revolutionary challenge that eventually resulted in substantial changes in the national government. For the first time, Mayan Indians, descendents of the builders of long abandoned Tikal, began joining revolutionary squads in the jungle to oppose the officials of Spanish ancestry still ruling the country. Earthquakes were the catalyst—an act of God that changed a government.

Recent earthquakes in Mexico City may have similar long-term consequences—not revolution, although that is possible, but the ruling PRI political party is now facing almost unsolvable economic and social problems in its capital city, the largest city in the world, with the highest unemployment rate and extensive and miserable slums. The destructive earthquake of 1985 seemed to expose the rulers of Mexico as bunglers and raised again the specter of election fraud. This has fostered the growth of opposition political parties of considerable credibility throughout the country. The aftermath of the quake— empty city blocks, destroyed buildings, schools without walls, abandoned hospitals, and thousands of homeless, is a constant reminder of a failed government.

It is all reminiscent of Nicaragua and Guatemala, and the Mexican people will surely also attribute the lack of reconstruction to corruption. The street comment has already been heard, "Now we will see who gets rich at the expense of us all." The Mexican people may no longer be tolerant of authorities who now wish to do something but cannot or do not.

Mexico continues to be a volatile country, though its ruling PRI party has never been seriously challenged. As the earthquake rubble is cleared Mexico will be a country to watch—in a land of volcanoes and earthquakes that have always done much more than just shake carved stones and bricks into the street.

CHAPTER FOUR

The Longest Crack

Cabo San Lucas, Baja California Sur, Mexico.

It was worrisome for awhile. An area astride the San Andreas fault north of Los Angeles had inexplicably risen ten inches in recent years. Similar swelling of the land had occurred prior to several earthquakes in California, and the United States Geological Survey (USGS), which made the announcement, expected nearby residents to be duly concerned about the "Palmdale Bulge." Bulging had preceded the early-morning 1971 San Fernando quake, but uplift may have occurred in 1914 within the Transverse Ranges with no earthquake following. It was a typical prediction dilemma. Robert Hamilton, chief of the USGS Office of Earthquake Studies, added that "we must not jump to conclusions based on the geodetic data alone." Reflecting California's relaxed attitude regarding earthquakes, very little was done. No one left town. Seven years later, the USGS quietly let it be known that a survey mistake had been made in measuring San Andreas fault elevations. There never was a bulge at Palmdale.

The name San Andreas is the distaff version of San Andres Valley, a flooded section of the fault used by San Francisco as a water-storage reservoir. No one knows when San Andreas Valley and fault became feminine. The valley was named in 1773 for the saint's day, San Andres Canada. Living in grass-thatched huts that only rustled when the earth shook, local Indians surely had no fear of the earthquakes that were probably ignored until Spanish Father Junipero Serra built his 21 missions from San Diego to San Rafael north of San Francisco, most of them located near the San Andreas fault line. Constructed of adobe brick, they suffered serious damage during repeated quakes, not necessarily the best demonstration for instilling the Indians' faith in their new God.

At San Juan Bautista, the mission built 150 years ago is on the edge of the active fault. After its completion, and tired of continually repairing cracks in the adobe walls that often appeared overnight, the fathers were pondering whether to build a new church or enlarge the old one when a series of strong earthquakes lasting twenty days jolted the area and most of the church collapsed. They rebuilt the old church and enlarged it.

The 1906 quake along the fault, felt mostly in San Francisco, also struck the mission hard, toppling outer walls weakened by ground water and knocking out a wall in the orphanage behind, nearly burying alive the children sleeping there.

The fault still slips and creeps as the Pacific plate drifts to the northwest along the edge of the North American continental plate. The movement of this 1,200-mile-long sliver of continental coast—some of its length beneath the sea, other portions forming crumpled mountains—has been going on for many millions of years, since the time when pre-historic animals roamed the earth. The edge of the Pacific plate would lock in place against the mainland crust for many centuries until built-up strain was suddenly released, allowing the crust to slip past the stationary rock and shake the continent on both sides of the fault. The fault in the area of Palmdale had not moved to any measurable extent since a local earthquake in 1857. Knowledge of a bulge was not taken lightly by the scientific community.

A large major earthquake along the San Andreas fault, such as the 1906 San Francisco quake (8.25 on the Richter scale), may take decades to develop, with ample opportunity for clues to appear and give warning. A warning is obviously important to major cities along the fault, where an earthquake registering 8 or more on the Richter scale with an epicenter in urban areas would cause considerable damage in San Francisco and Los Angeles, taking a heavy toll of human life.

Earthquakes measured on the Richter scale

San Andreas Fault, running upper left to lower right, Carrizo Plain, southern California.

mount quickly from a gentle shake to horror as the numbers change. An earthquake that would gently rock the bed on the Richter scale at 6 would probably collapse the house at Richter 7. Based on the amplitude of vibrations recorded on a seismograph, the scale is a fairly precise way of comparing the relative force of earthquakes. A tremor registering 6 on the scale is ten times greater than a 5, 100 times greater than a 4, and 1,000 times greater than a 3, the common shake that is barely felt. The seismograph and its Richter scale record the consequence of fault slippage—the magnitude of the earth's shake as the place moves. Rocks are somewhat elastic under pressure that deforms their structure, and when the pressure is suddenly released, as in a slipping fault, the rocks jerk loose in a "twang" like the snap of a rubber band.

Interviewed before he died in 1985 at his Altadena home in southern California, only a few miles from the San Andreas fault, Charles Richter expressed astonishment at the arrogance of developers building "earthquake-proof" structures. "They are putting up buildings in San Francisco and Los Angeles that they say will withstand a magnitude 8 earthquake. That is grossly misleading," said Richter. "What they are really sàying is that those buildings will withstand an event of that size which has an epicenter miles away. There are no buildings constructed by human beings that can withstand a magnitude 8 event right underneath them."

Downtown Los Angeles is 33 miles from the San Andreas fault. Downtown San Francisco is 5 miles away. No large city is astride the fault although the entire urban megatropolis extending from San Francisco to San Jose, where two million people reside, strad-

Union Street, San Francisco, after the 1906 earthquake. U.S. Geological Survey photo.

dles the fault for 50 miles. Virtually all the famed Silicon Valley computer manufacturing is centered on the fault.

The controversial Pacific Gas & Electric (PG&E) Company's Diablo Canyon nuclear power plant is 40 miles from San Andreas, but only 3 miles from a major undersea fault off-shore, a fault discovered after construction of the facility began. In issuing a license to oper-ate, the Federal Nuclear Regulatory Commis-sion did not hold a hearing on the danger from potential earthquakes, and the federal appeals court in affirming the NRC decision wrote that "the probability of any size earthquake occurring in San Luis Obispo (a nearby com-munity) in any given year is about one in 50. The probability that the two events (an earth-quake and nuclear accident) will occur con-temporaneously in a single week during the life of the plant is approximately one in 6.5 million."

Further south is the three-unit seaside San Onofre nuclear power plant operated by

Southern California Edison. It is about 50 miles distant from the San Andreas fault, where sci-entists predict a quake as powerful as 8.3 on the Richter scale within the next 30 years; 40 miles south of the still active Newport-Ingle-wood fault, responsible for a 1933 temblor that devastated the Long Beach area; and 5 miles from an underwater fault that hasn't moved yet. San Onofre has been constructed so each of its three reactors can withstand a 7.0 mag-nitude earthquake somewhere nearby.

Both power plants are located on the mov-ing Pacific plate, at sites considerably safer than the Bodega Bay peninsula originally proposed by PG&E for a nuclear power plant, a site reluctantly abandoned only after court orders were issued expressly prohibiting the com-pany from building at Bodega Bay directly over the San Andreas fault. Today a multimillion-dollar hole in the ground remains.

The anti-nuclear group, Alliance for Sur-vival, claims San Onofre is definitely vulner-able to major damage in a quake: "Being in

California and near faults, it just doesn't make sense to operate a nuclear plant."

AFTER THE DESTRUCTIVE and devastating 1933 Long Beach earthquake killed 115 people, local building codes and a new California state law required that schools be brought up to earthquake-resistant standards. Following the 1971 San Fernando Valley quake with 52 deaths and the dramatic collapse of a hospital wing and freeway overpasses, additional laws were enacted and engineers installed cables on state highway bridges to help prevent ground movement from pulling them apart.

Unreinforced buildings of brick block or stones held together with mortar and without steel reinforcement bars, buildings generally built before 1933, typify the kind of structures that the California Seismic Safety Commission would like to see reinforced or demol-ished to prevent loss of life or serious injury during a major earthquake. Many unreinforced buildings remain in use.

Only six cities in California—Santa Ana, Long Beach, Los Angeles, Santa Monica, Santa Rosa, and Sebastopol—have seismic safety ordinances that require building owners to bring structures up to earthquake safety standards or demolish them. A state law suggests that cities inventory buildings that do not meet earthquake-code standards, but the law lacks teeth because no state funding is available for cities to do inventories and few have. It is a beginning and opens the door for municipalities to pursue those hazardous buildings that are at best a negligible part of the tax base and could actually kill taxpayers.

In the absence of a state mandate, local jurisdictions have been left on their own and most have ignored the problem. When asked about potentially dangerous buildings, the city building department official of San Clemente, Walter Johnson, said, "God, I wouldn't know.

Downtown Los Angeles, California.

A collapsed overpass on California's north-south highway, Interstate 5, after the 1971 San Fernando Valley earthquake. U.S. Geological Survey photo.

It might be kind of interesting to do a survey on that."

There are about 8,000 listed, unreinforced, older masonry buildings in Los Angeles County that do not meet seismic safety codes. About 300 are public buildings, private schools, churches, theaters, and even restaurants that could quickly collapse during an expected moderate quake. A tremor of magnitude 8 centered on the San Andreas fault in southern California would produce heavy ground shaking for 30 seconds or more and possibly bring down every unsafe structure in the city with substantial loss of life. An earthquake of only 6 with a downtown epicenter could have equally devastating consequences.

The county and city politicians of Los Angeles over the years have attempted many times to solve the problem, short of requiring every building owner to level his buildings before an earthquake does it. At one time an ordinance was actually introduced that would have required landlords to mount a sign at the entrance to unreinforced structures informing all those who entered that they did so at their own risk and that during an earthquake the building might collapse at any time. It never became law.

Los Angeles city council members finally passed an ordinance in 1981 requiring structural upgrading of all older properties, and by 1986 about half of the 8,000 unreinforced buildings had been either demolished or structurally reinforced by steel beams or other methods to bring them up to code. It is expected that all the targeted buildings will be upgraded by 1992, including the many aging buildings in the downtown Broadway corridor.

There are several credible scenarios for earthquakes affecting Los Angeles. One is the oft-repeated prediction that sometime in the next 50 years, some say 30 (it might be tomorrow), there will be an 8.3 magnitude earthquake on the southern segment of the San Andreas fault.

Other possibilities include perhaps three magnitude 6.3 quakes over a period of years with a central business district or West Los Angeles or Long Beach epicenter. These might be triggered by other nearby faults quite numerous in the area, many not yet known. Moderately sized local earthquakes are quite common, such as the 1925 Santa Barbara quake (6.3), the 1933 Long Beach quake (6.3), the 1971 San Fernando Valley quake (6.4), the 1983 Coalinga quake (6.4), the 1984 Morgan Hill quake (6.2), and the 1986 Palm Springs and Orange County quakes (5.9).

Should a quake as violent as the 1906 San Francisco quake occur again, and it is probable according to USGS scientists, it is not so much the old that will be destroyed but much of the very new. As bridges and downtown highrises swing and sway, south of San Francisco the filled bayshore mudflats from

The San Andreas Fault and Coachella Canal, Chocolate Mountains and Imperial Valley, California.

Palo Alto to the airport and beyond may turn to quicksand, collapsing and breaking apart thousands of individual homes and condominiums in a dozen bayside subdivisions. The airport itself would suffer substantial damage to the runways, and miles of new row houses built astride the fault in Daly City would splinter and crumble as the shaking earth west of the fault shifted northward, perhaps for only a few feet but sufficiently far to kill thousands and cause property damage in the millions.

It is not known exactly how much the fault is slipping or where. It appears to vary from place to place, if recent measurements are correct. Some scientists claim the fault is slipping at a much faster pace than in past years. Some investigators indicated that land seaward of the fault is moving northward at an average rate of perhaps 4½ inches per year, or one mile in 25,000 years, twice as fast as previous measurements had shown. Neither a slower nor a faster average rate would indicate an earthquake would occur soon; the timing and destructiveness of a future quake would be the result of how suddenly the fault shifts and how close to the major population centers the shift occurs.

Current high-technology laser-satellite measuring technics, used to calculate the time it takes for faint radio waves from distant quasars to reach the earth, have replaced cumbersome ground surveying methods along the fault and enabled scientists to obtain highly accurate measurements of the drifting continental edge.

Movement of the San Andreas fault as little as the width of a thumb is calculated by listening to quasars six sextillion miles away. When changes in the time it takes for signals to reach California antennas are measured, it is determined that California west of the fault has moved, since astronomers assume that the quasars are fixed in the sky. Using radio signals from space, measurements have been made of the distance between the Goldstone Tracking Station in the eastern Mojave Desert and the Jet Propulsion Laboratory in Pasadena on the moving western side of the San Andreas fault. The tracking station and the laboratory moved more than 5 inches farther apart over a recent three-year period. During the same years another section of the fault south of the San Gabriel Mountains may have moved apart 8 inches.

Measurements made since 1973 indicate that San Diego in southern California has been moving closer toward the state capital, Sacramento, in northern California at the rate of 3.6 inches a year (although some San Diego politicians may deny the movement). Surveys of the Imperial Valley fault crossing rich farmlands north of the Mexican border show a shift of 5 inches a year measured over a 37-year period. The Imperial Valley fault has jerked a bit during sudden shifts in recent years, causing considerable earthquake damage in the Brawley agricultural community.

The Pacific plate determines the future life of everything upon it, yet economic pressures and wishful thinking run contrary to good common sense as the continent continues to be deformed beneath our feet. Most of the plate movement along the San Andreas fault occurs over long time spans, years and decades, that have never been recorded by even the most sensitive seismic terrestrial instruments. Not until the radio waves from distant quasars were measured was it confirmed that Los Angeles is indeed moving closer to San Francisco—Los Angeles being on the northward drifting Pacific plate and San Francisco on the relatively stationary continental plate. Whether San Francisco will still be there when Los Angeles arrives is another matter for conjecture.

It is easy to ignore the consequences of what cannot be felt. Unless the land has jerked a bit, few are concerned about geologic forces changing the shape of a future California that will not be seen in our lifetimes. Residents in the eastern United States have noted, however, that the California lifestyle, as well as the geology, is somewhat more exotic on the west side of the San Andreas fault compared with the rest of the continent. Both the people and the rocks in West Hollywood are considerably different from those in Bakersfield.

One of our favored self-deceptions is that disaster is something that happens elsewhere—to someone else. Airliners crash, bridges wash out with cars on them, tornados hit, volcanoes erupt, and earthquakes shake, communicating the shifting of the earth in ominous fashion. Still, like moths to a flame, drawn to the fire that will destroy them, we stay near, living on the edge, feeling somehow that the agony of death and destruction will occur elsewhere. Very few residents have moved away from California because the state shakes now and then as it changes shape. Being near death and not knowing when it may occur may provide an extra load of excitement to native Californians.

There is also another ingredient. From TV-saturated suburbanites to corporate chairmen to the bearded guy on the Harley-Davidson, we may all be starved for good, old-fashioned, "primitive" emotion. Beyond being overwhelmed by events we cannot control, there seems to be a need to stand near catastrophic events, just as we slow down to view freeway wrecks in the other lane. What better events to fill us with fear and trembling than forces as fantastically powerful as volcanoes and earthquakes, providing us with at least a renewed sense of awe and wonder.

Denying seismophobia is a habit of California residents living on one side or the other of the mighty San Andreas fault, especially so when water sloshes back and forth in the

swimming pool. It's a matter of adapting to the rattle of glasses on the shelf, the sight of tilted picture frames in the morning, and new cracks in the ceiling. Liquor store owners have learned to pen in their bottles behind wire mesh to avoid having valuable blends somersault from the shelf. Supermarket owners abhor a gentle rocking in bed at night, because they know from previous shaky evenings that upon opening the market in the morning they will be greeted by a messy mix of syrup, catsup, and liquid soap combined with almost everything else for sale in the store.

Maverick civic boosters for the valley town of Hollister, south of San Francisco and astride San Andreas, where minor shudders of the loamy soil occur every day, have devised a catchy slogan to describe what the Chamber of Commerce avoids mentioning in civic promotions: "The Earthquake Capital of the World." USGS scientists have installed 275 seismographs in surrounding pastures and

Earthquake damage, Mission San Juan Capistrano, California.

farmland to record the shaking place as it drifts toward San Francisco, this year only 85 miles away.

Other residents think of ways to make money from the notoriety, such as carnival rides that would shake passengers according to the Richter scale until they fell out. In nearby San Juan Bautista is the Fault Line Restaurant, where a previous owner, calling himself Sam Andreas, gave free meals to patrons when a quake of 3.5 or better struck while they were eating. The idea of having an "earthquake festival" to attract tourists in the summer is yet to be realized, however.

As far as most residents are concerned, Hollister is their home. The earth may move but they will not. It is a normal reaction, says UCLA sociologist Ralph Turner. "We don't worry about threats or risks unless they are highly probable and imminent. When we are confronted with threats about which we can do nothing, we react by denial. It keeps our sanity."

The constant quakes can be frightening to many who jump out of bed at the slightest quiver. In southern California, when a second quake of 5.3 shook Orange County only five days after a quake of 5.9, hospital officials reported that a 55-year-old woman died of a heart attack she suffered at her home during the earthquake.

Apart from the possible emotional high from living where things are happening—or about to—California residents highly value the social and economic advantages of staying where they are, compared to the risks of a potentially disastrous event that may not occur. Short-term advantages are easily calculated, and long-term risks are easily ignored. Yet the dangerous events at Mexico City and Mt. St. Helens were not very far away. Measured against geologic time, San Francisco in 1906 was this morning. Tomorrow may be just hours from now. The time and date of the next major quake are unknown, but it will occur.

Earth scientists predict a severe local quake in California within the next few years, possibly 5 to 6 or greater on the Richter scale, resulting from a sudden shifting movement of the San Andreas fault in Cholame Valley, about halfway between Los Angeles and San Francisco. Expected to center on the small town of Parkfield straddling San Andreas, the fault shift could well lead to the anticipated "big one," triggering a quake measuring 8 or

more in the Los Angeles metropolitan basin 200 miles south.

Residents of Parkfield seem not too worried over living in a potentially very exciting place. A Parkfield teacher recalls, "My relatives have lived out here for 100 years, and the worst they had to do was put their chimneys back up." Longtime resident Donalee Thompson remembers a 1934 earthquake that threw her against the wall during a school play, and then again in 1966, hanging onto the kitchen door as dishes crashed about her. "I'm afraid of earthquakes," she says, "but anywhere you go, there's an element of danger. In cities you have murders and muggings. Life's a gamble, any way you look at it." Earthquakes do inspire "a sense of awe when you think about how minute a human being is, and how much earth a moderate earthquake will move."

USGS academics in Menlo Park were thrust into public consciousness when the press began to take volcanoes and earthquakes much more seriously following the 1971 San Fernando Valley quake. The long crack called San Andreas became the most closely watched segment of any earthquake fault in the world. Extensive arrays of monitoring equipment were set up near sensitive parts of the fault, on both sides of Hollister in northern California, in the Parkfield area, and straddling each side of the fault complex in southern California where a high-tech laser distance-ranging network measures actual strains accumulating in the crust. It is an attempt to get away from the hypothetical and predict the actual event.

Following the successful prediction of Mt. St. Helens's frightening eruption in time to save the lives of many loggers and campers who otherwise would have been within the prohibited danger zone, theoretical earth science became real-time geology. Mt. St. Helens became one of the most photographed and studied volcanoes on any continent.

Scientists have long hypothesized future quakes along the San Andreas fault by estimating the recurrence time from the historic quake of 1857—about 140 years. That would make a 50 percent likelihood of another quake along the southern end of the fault sometime in the next 30 years. The forecasted quake would cause between 3,000 and 13,000 deaths, depending upon whether it occurred at night or during busy com-

The tilted geologic structures of San Pedro Point, Daly City, California. The San Andreas Fault enters the Pacific Ocean nearby.

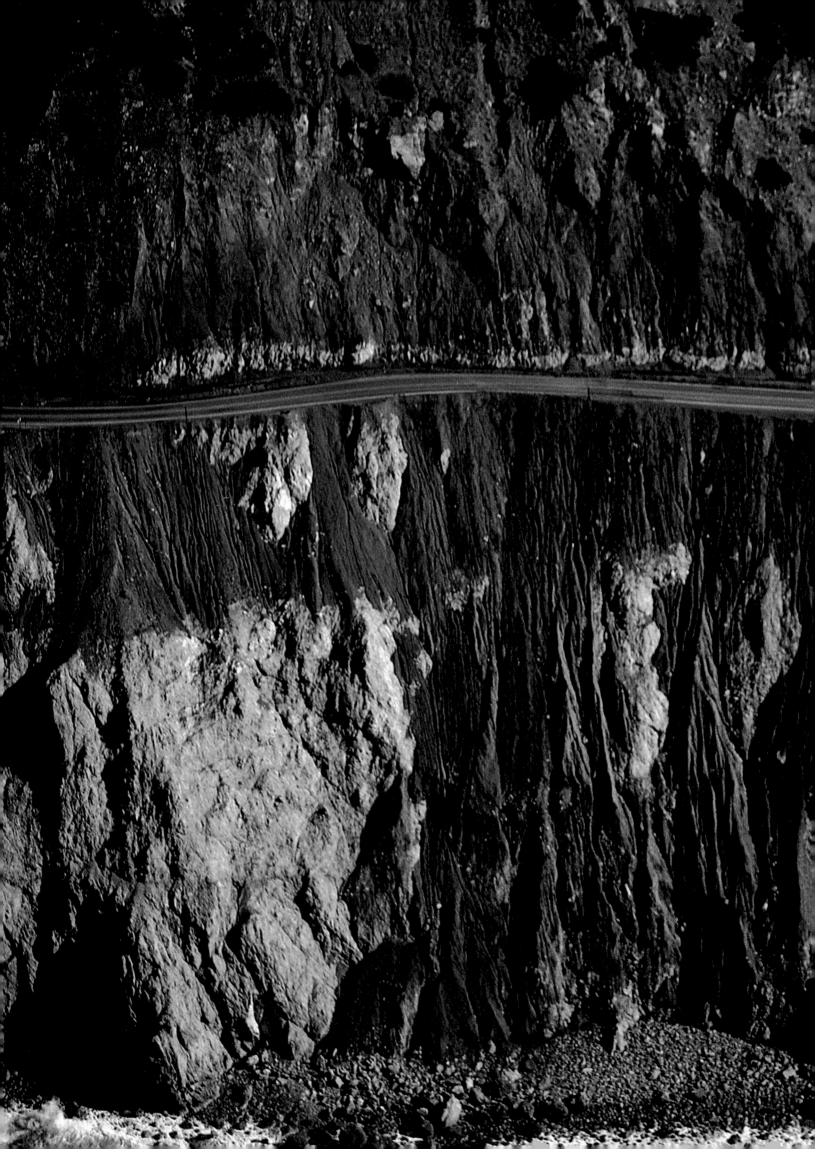

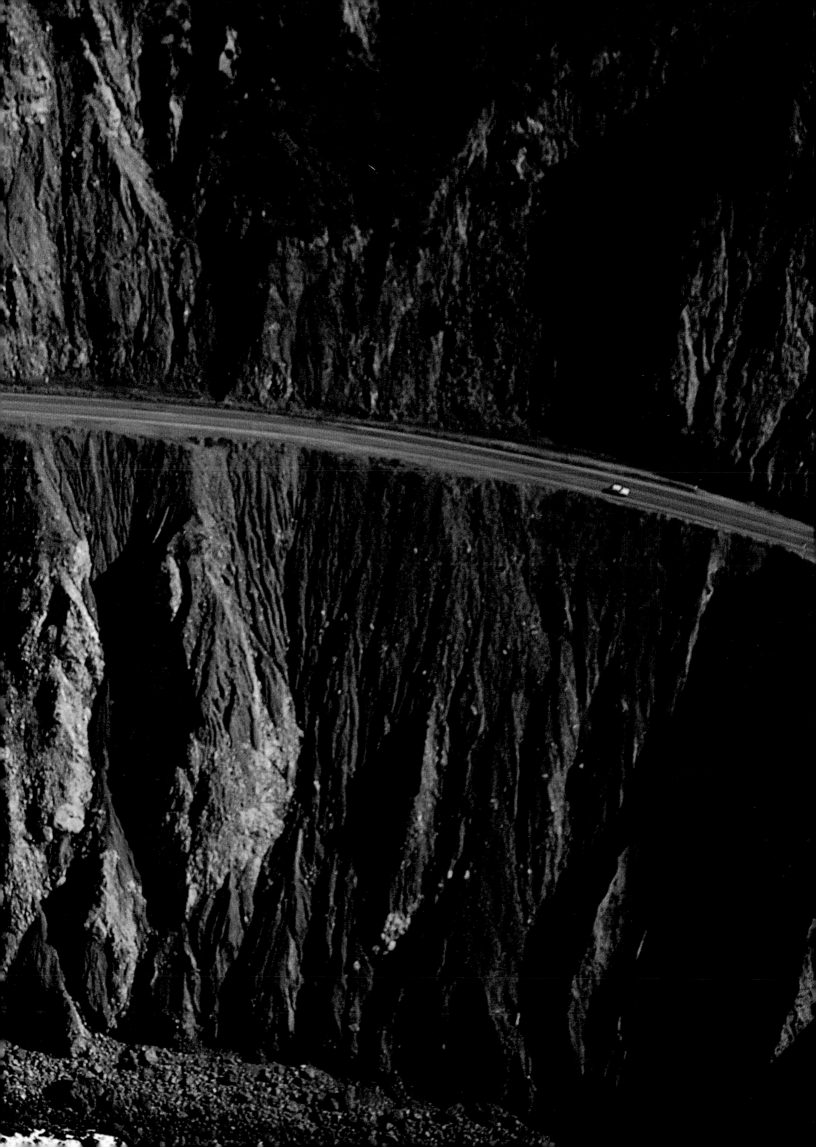

Westin Hotel, Puerto Vallarta, at the entrance to the Gulf of California across from Cabo San Lucas, Mexico. The rocks here are similar in structure and age to those near Tomales Bay, California.

muter hours with crowded freeways and surface streets. Californians will be safest at home in bed. Or standing in a doorway.

As THE FLOOR of the Pacific Ocean spreads outward toward the continents, fed by newly erupted volcanic materials from mid-ocean rifts within the oceanic floor, the easternmost edge of the ocean plate is pushed into and under the North American continent offshore of Mexico, Oregon, Washington, and British Columbia. The virtually continuous plate movement occurs over the curved surface of the earth, moving in a northwesterly direction and pulling the lands west of the San Andreas fault crack in the same direction. This average slide of several inches a year has occurred for millions of years, hundreds of centuries, and is an integral part

of the movement of drifting continents and ocean floors over the entire surface of the earth.

This longest crack, extending from coastal Mexico to northern California, is not a continuous straight crack but, for most of its length, rather like a flaking edge of slumping mud, with adjacent fractures and breaks, sometimes at right angles, relieving the underground stresses in unpredictable directions. It is not a single fault; it is many cracks and fissures, characteristic of a crumbling slice of dry cake, rather than the edge of a continent.

The well-known name, San Andreas fault, actually applies to the crack only in California north of Los Angeles, where its shaky behavior was sufficiently strong in 1906 to remind San Franciscans quite forcibly that their city was built on the edge of a danger-

Overleaf: Highway 1 crosses the Devils Slide, Daly City, California.

ous fault system. Their city has continued to shake at irregular intervals over the years.

Across San Francisco Bay is the Hayward fault, which bisects Oakland. The adjacent Calaveras and Sargent faults branch off in the Santa Clara Valley, where a strong 1982 quake emptied market shelves in Morgan Hill. Fault movement is a slow creep in Hollister, where the crack can be easily located by noting offset concrete curb lines. Further south, in the Temblor Range, the fault is a straight line for miles across rolling fields of weeds and wheat.

The extreme northern section of the crack in California mirrors the southernmost portion in Mexico as Tomales Bay appears to lengthen and widen. During the 1906 San Francisco earthquake, roads and fences in many areas that straddled the fault were offset several yards, while the road crossing the head of Tomales Bay was offset almost 21 feet, the maximum horizontal displacement recorded. The ground west of the fault, as in all movements along the fault, was moved northward, and it would be of interest to know what distance Tomales Bay was lengthened and widened. It may have been considerable if the Gulf of California in Mexico at the southern end is any example of what can occur.

Each end of the fault crack terminates where the crustal break is intercepted and consumed by the advancing ocean floor. Here the fault dips beneath the continents. Where this subduction occurs, friction generated beneath the continental crust produces molten rock and active volcanoes in weak parts of the crust and its associated mountain ranges: in the Pacific Northwest, the Cascades; far to the south a string of volcanoes across central Mexico—Colima, Pericutín, Popocatepetl, Orizaba, and El Chichón. An estimated ten million tons of volcanic ash and sulfuric gases spewed out of El Chichón in 1982, one of the most violent eruptions in the world since the 1815 eruption of Tambora in Indonesia. During the next year, New England shivered under what has been called the "year without a summer." In Mexico it snowed in June and the corn crop failed, smothered under a blanket of ash.

Subducting plates beneath the continent caused magma to erupt from the weak crustal surface at Mt. St. Helens in 1980. In 1945, the shifting fault extending completely across Mexico from the Pacific to the Gulf pro-

duced Pericutín, a new volcano in a Mexican cornfield. The sliding plate continues to keep central Mexican volcanoes fuming and the countryside shaking. Even Mexico City is not immune from earthquakes originating deep beneath the ocean where the longest crack begins a couple of hundred miles offshore. Recent records of earthquakes of 1.5 magnitude and larger along the San Andreas fault complex show the largest concentrations of quakes are located undersea off the northern California coast and at the head of the Gulf of California. If proper instrumentation were in place in Mexico, the shaking coastal ocean floor off Acapulco might indicate well in advance when another major earthquake in Mexico would occur.

The long crack marking the slip-joint where moving sections of the ocean plate slide to the northwest is easily followed from above in low-flying aircraft. At Cabo San Lucas, the extreme southern point of Baja, opposite Mazatlán, the continent has broken apart, allowing the Pacific Ocean waters to enter into sheltered coves and also attracting tourists and mating whales to the protected Gulf of California.

The gulf is a peaceful and quiet sea hiding undersea cliffs that drop abruptly into deep water. It forms an unseen deep trench below the surface that continues southeastward along the Mexican coast toward the undersea junction west of Acapulco, where the Pacific plate slides past the Cocos plate. Immediately south of the Mexican border, the fault crack is the long, slender, and very deep gulf where Colorado River waters drain into the sea, far south, however, from where the river's original delta began spreading many hundreds of years ago in California's Imperial Valley.

Baja California still slides to the northwest along the coastal California landscape, as it has for an estimated 30 million years, with Cabo San Lucas marking the last coastal remnant of the breakaway crust in Mexico. Other identifying fragments have been located in the north, where geologists have compared the rocks on Montera Mountain along the fault south of San Francisco and found them substantially the same in mineral content and age as rocks along the shore of the Mexican mainland at Puerto Vallarta. Montera on the fault is an unusual place on earth, where it is possible to leap a thousand miles in geologic time with a single jump

Shore at Ixtapa, Zihautanejo, Mexico, where rocks are geologically similar to those on Montara Mountain, south of San Francisco. Ixtapa is the nearest landfall to the ocean floor epicenter of the 1985 Mexico City earthquake.

across the San Andreas fault. As the fault continues sliding northward, inexorably pushed by the expanding Pacific plate, a prediction may be made that Los Angeles will, in time, be alongside San Francisco, and a new, somewhat narrow continent will appear off the coasts of northern California, the Pacific Northwest, and Canada. It remains to be seen what country it will belong to.

A deep ocean trench adjoins the edges of Asia and the North and South American continents for the entire Pacific Ocean circumference with one exception, coastal California, where no ocean trench exists. The deep trench extends into the Gulf of California, only to end where the Colorado River delta has filled the upper gulf with silt. Until about 30 million years ago a continuous trench existed up the coast of what is California today, ending at the Juan de Fuca plate to complete the Pacific circle. The trench

still exists; it is now beneath the great western desert and plain basin, extending from the Gulf into the Imperial Valley, Arizona, the Carson Sink, Nevada, Death Valley, and Utah. Extensive layers of sedimentary deposits are evidence that a trench once existed in these arid lands, a trench much like the present trough along the west coast of Mexico. Imperial Valley farmers today plow these sedimentary deposits, irrigated by water from the Colorado River, draining a continent slowly moving west, crumpling mountains between the ancient plains.

Maybe 30 million years ago, according to some estimates, the easternmost spreading rift in the Pacific collided with the North American continental plate near coastal central Mexico, began pushing the Cocos plate beneath what is now Mexico, and pushed the eastern landform of the old trench northward, forcing its separation from the

Rocks near Dillon Beach in northern California are similar to those south of Puerto Vallarta, Mexico.

North American continent and creating the San Andreas fault. Sometime in the future it could be a trench again or a wide inland sea with deep-water access to the Pacific. California could be a new continent. It was a lake long ago—it could be an ocean again. Palm Springs could have beaches and a seaport. Sand from the old ocean days is still there.

California might split off in another quite unexpected place, along fault complexes crumbling the Klamath Mountains inland of Cape Mendocino, where the San Andreas fault creeps into the ocean off the northern coast. Or, as is most probable, it might happen along the transverse Garlock fault already in place, splitting southern California from northern in a crack reaching from Cape Concepción at Santa Barbara into Death Valley, already below sea level and awaiting the new flood. In any case, the future will reveal a quite different landscape.

CHAPTER FIVE

The Drifting Wrinkled West

Sierra Nevada escarpment near Lake Crowley, California.

There were no seismographs in place to measure the shock, but by every description the 1872 earthquake in Owens Valley, at the base of the eastern Sierra slope, was the most severe earthquake to strike California in recorded history. By some estimates 100 times greater than the 1906 San Francisco earthquake, the shock virtually demolished the small settlement of Lone Pine, killing a reported 29 residents in the sparsely settled community. Without warning, fault scarps appeared, extending for miles along the valley's western side, sections of land dropping 20 feet or more, tearing apart cabins and smashing public buildings. Huge rockfalls were triggered in Yosemite Valley, brick walls were cracked 300 miles away, and windows rattled in Salt Lake City.

Fifty-two of the 59 structures in Lone Pine were destroyed. Every building constructed of brick, stone, and adobe collapsed on that frosty night in March, killing most residents instantly. Sixteen were buried in a common grave since they had no relatives nearby, most being recent immigrants from Ireland, Chile, France, Mexico, and the eastern states who were working as farmhands, cowboys, and miners.

Geologists claim the Sierra moved about 20 feet horizontally that night and in a few moments rose upward several feet while the Owens Valley floor dropped 20 feet. The Lone Pine earthquake was monstrous, but the rumbling and roaring that occurred in Owens Valley around 2:25 A.M. on April 6, awakening everyone only a few minutes before the full force of the earthquake struck, is probably best described by the most eloquent writer of the Sierra, John Muir, who was living in Yosemite Valley at the time. His description of the 1872 quake, as felt in Yosemite, is the only known eye-witness account. Muir's cabin was 65 miles from the epicenter near Lone Pine.

The shocks were so violent and varied, and succeeded one another so closely, that I had to balance myself carefully in walking as if on the deck of a ship among waves, and it seemed impossible that the high cliffs of the Valley could escape being shattered. In particular, I feared that the sheer-fronted Sentinel Rock, towering above my cabin, would be shaken down, and I took shelter back of a large yellow pine, hoping that it might protect me from at least the smaller outbounding boulders. For a minute or two the shocks became more and more violent—flashing horizontal thrusts mixed with a few twists and battering, explosive, upheaving jolts—as if Nature were wrecking her Yosemite temple, and getting ready to build a still better one.

It was a calm moonlight night, and no sound was heard for the first minute or so, save low, muffled, underground bubbling rumblings, and the whispering and rustling of the agitated trees, as if Nature were holding her breath. Then, suddenly, out of the strange silence and strange motion there came a tremendous roar. The Eagle Rock on the south wall, about a half mile up the Valley, gave way and I saw it falling in thousands of the great boulders I had so long been studying, pouring to the Valley floor in a free curve luminous from friction, making a terribly sublime spectacle—an arc of glowing, passionate fire, fifteen hundred feet span, as true in form and as serene in beauty as a rainbow in the midst of the stupendous, roaring rock-storm. The sound was so tremendously deep and broad and earnest, the whole earth like a living creature seemed to have at last found a voice and to be calling her sister planets. In trying to tell something of the size of this awful sound it seems to me that if all the thunder of all the storms I have ever heard were condensed into one roar it would not equal this rock-roar at the birth of a mountain talus.

The first severe shocks were soon over, and eager to examine the new-born talus I ran up the Valley in the moonlight and climbed upon it before the huge blocks, after their fiery flight, had come to complete rest. They were slowly settling into their places, chafing, grating against one another, groaning, and whispering; but no motion was visible except in a stream of small fragments pattering down the face of the cliff. A cloud of dust particles, lighted by the moon, floated out across the whole breadth of the Valley, forming a ceiling that lasted until after sunrise, and the air was filled with the odor of crushed Douglas spruces from a grove that had been mowed down and mashed like weeds.

After a second startling shock, about half-past three o'clock, the ground continued to tremble gently, and smooth, hollow rumbling sounds, not always distinguishable from the rounded, bumping, explosive tones of the falls, came from deep in the mountains in a northern direction.

Shortly after sunrise a low, blunt, muffled rumbling, like distant thunder, was followed by another series of shocks, which, though not nearly so severe as the first, made the cliffs and domes tremble like jelly, and the big pines and oaks thrill and swish and wave their branches with startling effect.

During the third severe shock (that same morning) the trees were so violently shaken that the birds flew out with frightened cries. In particular, I noticed two robins flying in terror from a leafless oak, the branches of which swished and quivered as if struck by a heavy battering-ram. Exceedingly interesting were the flashing and quivering of the elastic needles of the pines in the sunlight and the waving up and down of the branches while the trunks stood rigid.

It was long before the Valley found perfect rest. The rocks trembled more or less every day for over two months, and I kept a bucket of water on my table to learn what I could of the movements. The blunt thunder in the depths of the mountains was usually followed by sudden jarring, horizontal thrusts from the northward, often succeeded by twisting, upjolting movements. More than a month after the first great shock, when I was standing on a fallen tree up the Valley near Lamon's winter cabin, I heard a distinct bubbling thunder from the direction of Tenaya Canyon. The air was perfectly still, not the faintest breath of wind perceptible, and a fine, mellow, sunny hush pervaded everything, in the midst of which came that subterranean thunder. Then, while we gazed and listened, came the corresponding shocks, distinct as if some mighty hand had shaken the ground. After the sharp horizontal jars died away, they were followed by a gentle rocking and undulating of the ground so distinct that Carlo (the dog) looked at the log on which he was standing to see who was shaking it. It was the season of flooded meadows and the pools about me, calm as sheets of glass, were suddenly thrown into low ruffling waves.

Owens Valley and Lone Pine are 123 miles north of Palmdale and the San Andreas fault, where urban smears on the Mohave desert are first seen when driving northeast out of Los Angeles. This is the beginning of basin-and-range country extending a thousand miles east to Wyoming—the wrinkled west of upthrust mountains separated by arid valleys that were the last natural obstacles to early immigrant wagon trains headed west. Within this disheveled landscape is the Great Salt Lake Desert, Donner Pass in the Sierra

Whitney Portal, Sierra Nevada east escarpment near Lone Pine, California.

where travelers caught in a winter storm ate some of each other before crossing the mountain summit, and appropriately named Death Valley on the Nevada border, 282 feet below sea level and the lowest point in the United States.

Mt. Whitney, highest point in the United States (14,495 feet) is only 88 miles due west of Death Valley, across the Inyo Mountains and directly above Lone Pine at the crest of the impressive eastern escarpment of the Sierra Nevada. Below Whitney are the Alabama Hills edging Owens Valley, a dramatic assortment of eroded rocks featured in numerous Hollywood cowboy films. They are the top of a bedrock scarp buried in over 9,000 feet of gravel, sand, and rock debris deposited over millions of years. The buried bedrock bottom of Owens Valley adjoining the Alabama scarp is 6,000 feet below sea level at Lone Pine, and year by year the valley surface drops farther, occasionally in sudden breaks, more often in a gradual subsidence noticed only by seismic instruments.

About 150 million years ago—when shallow seas covered the mountain peaks that were then below sea level—the crest of the Sierra was the edge of the continent, but as the Pacific Ocean floor pushed into and partially beneath the continent, crunching against the westward-drifting continental plate, the embryonic mountains were upthrust almost three miles above sea level. As the eastern Owens Valley continues to drop, the Sierra continues to thrust upward, not much, possibly only an inch or so over 100 years (apparently it's been slowing down over the last few million). As the crest rises, the jagged peaks with embedded ancient ocean fossils tilt westward.

The crunch between the plates persists, and earthquakes continue to disturb this convoluted landscape. In 1978, a serious earthquake shook the area. Again in 1980, long after Lone Pine was shaken to the ground, earthquakes became front-page news, not because the faulted landscape had been altogether quiet since 1872, but in the intervening years thousands of people had moved onto the eastern Sierra foothills and a major winter resort city with every urban amenity was constructed within and on the rim of an ancient volcanic caldera. When Mammoth Lakes skiers were shaken, it was news—reporters, scientists, and condominium owners arrived simultaneously to ascertain the damage.

The 1980 tremor in the Mammoth Lakes area, a 6 on the Richter scale, was much less powerful than John Muir experienced, but the shaking did trigger rockfalls in Yosemite, 40 miles away. The Mammoth Lake caldera area was severely shaken that year with 5.9 and 5.2 quakes, neither as strong as the 1980 tremor. The quake arrived on a sunny Sunday spring morning in May, with a jarring, lurching movement accompanied by the tinkle of broken windows and clatter of falling china, pots, and pans in every kitchen. Books were thrown from library shelves, and bricks thudded down from broken chimneys.

A strange muffled thunder was heard as the ground ceased shaking. Along the mountain front and within narrow canyons, rockfalls and avalanches added to the confusion of a disrupted and frightened community. Clouds of dust rose from the surrounding mountains and enveloped high peaks in a smog-like haze. At the nearby hot springs, geysers began spurting superheated water up to 30 feet high. New boiling pools appeared and many existing hot springs and pools became hotter and stayed that way. A fisherman on Lake Crowley saw great bubbles of gas disgorge from the water as waves rippled the surface. It was the largest earthquake in 40 years and was followed by 600 aftershocks.

Arriving like aftershocks, seismologists, geologists, and geophysicists came to town, most significantly volcanologists, all carrying specialized instruments to measure and probe and look at the earth's ruptured surface, note displacements, rockfalls, and avalanches, stick their feet and fingers in the hot springs, and attempt to determine the extent of geological and geothermal change.

THE UPPER OWENS VALLEY and Mono Lake region appeared to be undergoing significant alteration after years of being still. The mountains had risen so little that any difference could not be measured. The valley floor had dropped without much disturbance to those using only the surface, but except for concerned scientists, only passing thought had been given to the significance of faults

Hot Springs Creek near Long Valley caldera, California.

along the eastern Sierra front, faults on both sides of Owens Valley that extended deep within the earth to a depth of many miles where molten magma was able to flow upward in weak sections of bedrock.

Epicenters of the largest temblors were clearly along the ancient Long Valley caldera rim even though obvious surface ruptures were not, and when seismographs were installed throughout the Mammoth Lakes area, underground movement of magma more than four miles beneath the earth's surface was detected and geologists began to consider possible volcanic activity. When precise elevation measurements indicated a rising bulge in Long Valley and vicinity, carefully worded warnings were issued that indicated the possibilities of a much more dramatic and deadly event, not just another earthquake.

The Mammoth Lakes-Mono Craters-Long Valley volcanic history features many erup-

tions like those in Hawaii where it is usually permissible to drive up and watch, but the main Mono Basin eruptions were explosive, and dominant rock types east of the Sierra are commonly associated with violent volcanic eruptions. The two phenomena, earthquakes and volcanic eruptions, may have a common derivation as any casual glance at the chain of volcanic craters, earthquake cracks, and fault scarps among the cinder cones in the Mono Basin will confirm.

Mono Basin faults may indeed be sufficiently deep to intercept magma encroaching into subsurface cracks, but shifting faults may also relate directly to the subducting Juan de Fuca oceanic plate, a part of the Pacific plate off the coast of northern California and Oregon. Just as this oceanic plate is the fundamental cause of volcanic activity in the Cascade Range, the possible influence of the Juan de Fuca plate on increasing magma injection into the dormant rift system of the Mono Basin is not to be discounted.

It was 700,000 years ago that the volcano where Mammoth Lakes Resort is located exploded in a cataclysmic eruption 200 times greater than the 1980 eruption of Mt. St. Helens. It covered 450 square miles from Mono Lake to Chalfant Valley north of Bishop with a thick layer of volcanic ash, locally known as Bishop Tuff. It was less than 600 years ago that Mono Dome, less than three miles north of Mammoth Lakes Village, erupted, and about 500 years ago that lava flowed from an active vent in Negit Island in the center of Mono Lake. Tree-ring counts and active carbon-14 measurements of plant matter reveal that craters just south of the lake all erupted in a major way about 580 years ago.

The Owens Valley-Mono Lake area is one of three geologically active California regions (the others are Mt. Shasta and Mt. Lassen) being studied by the United States Geologi-

cal Survey's volcanic hazards program. Historically, volcanic activity in the Mono Basin does resemble events at Mt. St. Helens, and a series of historic eruptions along a 25-mile linear zone extending from Mammoth Mountain to Mono Lake has been catalogued by geologists, most of them minor in their effect on surrounding terrain when only native peoples lived in the basin, others throwing out pumice and ash as far as 60 miles distant. There is no evidence that this pattern of eruptive events, at an historical average of one eruption per century, will not occur again. It was during the last ice age that the most colossal eruption to ever occur in the west split open Long Valley. Air-borne ash from this eruption has been positively identified as falling to earth as far away as Nebraska. It was more violent than the decapitation of Mt. Mazama that created Crater Lake.

Evidence indicates a pool of magma about 12 miles in extent still exists beneath Mono

Cinder cone on eastern slope of Mt. Bachelor, south of Mt. St. Helens, in the Cascade Range near Bend, Oregon.

Mt. Lassen, Cascade Range, Mt. Lassen National Park, California.

Craters. It's several miles down and slowly migrating toward the surface. No one can forecast, using the very preliminary evidence now available, a future eruption in the Mono Basin. However, as the thermal hot springs at Whitmore and Hot Creek boil even more furiously, bubbling fumaroles high on Mammoth Mountain continue to warm winter skiers, and geysers at Casa Diablo erupt with increasing force, it behooves thoughtful observers to realize that a lull in earthquakes or dropping fault scarps is but a quiet chapter in a far from finished volcanic story with no end. A quiet week in Mono country may be only a temporary respite from violent weeks in the future.

Geophysicists John Rundle of the Sandia National Laboratories in New Mexico and James Whitcomb of the University of Colorado's Cooperative Institute for Research in Environmental Sciences both outlined theories in 1983 that called for a volcanic erup-

tion at Mammoth Lakes within the next few years if molten rock continues to thrust upward into an underground reservoir near the surface.

The two scientists were careful to emphasize that they were not actually predicting a volcanic eruption at the popular ski resort 180 miles east of San Francisco, saying, "Our work is more of an envelope of probabilities, based on the assumption that our theoretical construction is correct, which we don't know, and that the amount of molten rock injection in the future is known, which it is right now."

Their calculations suggest that when molten rock fills the elevated storage chamber, there is a point when the overhead rock ceiling will break and lava will then burst out in some sort of an eruption.

Other scientists say it is one possibility, but by no means the only possibility, but scientists have also found evidence suggesting that in past centuries a series of earthquakes shattered the earth's surface, allowing large, vertical sheets of molten rock to squeeze toward the surface, such as the long, linear crack developing along the southern edge of Long Valley, a few miles south of the resort village. According to USGS reports, it would be quite possible for an earthquake to trigger an eruption of the slumbering volcano with few advance warning signs.

KNOWN BY THE PAIUTE INDIANS as the "burnt land," the Mono Basin region is receiving continuous study because the area is considered among the most likely areas for eruptions in the near future. Even aging Mammoth Mountain itself is not entirely cool. Fumes rise from a fumarole on the south flank and a hot spot near chairlift 3. Hot springs still flow within the collapsed caldera, heated by magma within a few miles of the surface.

Active development of geothermal activity for power is underway. Dan Miller, a Denver-based USGS geologist, says, "There is no way of knowing whether eruptions will occur in days, decades or, perhaps, hundreds of years. Nor can the size and exact nature of the eruptions be predicted. It is certain there will be eruptions."

The vice president of Mammoth Properties, concerned about press coverage reporting that the resort village was built in a volcanic caldera that may erupt, said the company will overcome the problems of past earthquakes and the devastating consequences of volcano warnings by government geologists and media coverage of their findings. The *Los Angeles Times* reported, "Some townspeople pointed out that Mammoth Lake is in no more danger, probably less, than southern California is from a major earthquake." Whether it was the gasoline shortage, the drought years, or earthquake and eruptions warnings, each time there was an

Mono Lake volcanic island, Lee Vining, California.

exodus from the town. "There is always a revolving door of people coming and going," said businessmen. "It's not an easy area to live in and own property."

Local folks, permanent residents in the resort village, dependent on tourism and condominium resales, say the statements that Mammoth is imminently threatened by a major earthquake and volcanic eruption are much ado about nothing. Scientists would say the facts are somewhere in between: there is much ado about quite a bit, though, as *Sunset* magazine put it, "probably not enough to keep you off the ski slopes." In just 48 hours during May 1980, the area was rocked by four Richter scale 6 earthquakes, alerting geologists to a possibly significant change in the area's underground behavior. Surveys of the Long Valley caldera paralleling U.S. Highway 395, passing Mammoth, determined quite definitely that a 10-inch uplifting of the earth's surface had occurred. This development, combined with more tremors felt throughout the area plus new thermal activity in the hot springs, prompted the USGS office to issue a "Notice of Potential Volcanic Hazard" in May 1982, the lowest of three levels of hazard warning issued by the geological service. The hazard warning would remain in effect until something more hazardous happened, or nothing happened at all.

The USGS in its Circular 877 said: "Recent earthquakes, ground deformation, and increased fumarolic activity in the vicinity of Mammoth Lakes . . . have increased the concern over the possibility of a volcanic eruption in the near future, although no one can yet reliably predict either that there will be an eruption, or the time, scale, or specific site if an eruption does occur."

Residents of Mammoth Lakes Village reacted with outrage. Realtors did their own predicting, claiming that the news would destroy their profitable condominium market. Banks worried about foreclosed condo resales, averaging about 25 units per year even then. Shopkeepers complained that the warning was not justified and was driving tourists away; after all, when was the last eruption? General contractors and ski-lift operators did not want to hear volcanoes even mentioned.

More and more scientists converged on the Mono Basin to set up sensitive instruments to measure the shakes and bulge, but as summer passed into fall, many Mammoth

Earthquake crack near Mammoth Lakes, California.

residents quit saying "never" and began to worry about "when?"

Federal and state officials, testifying at a public meeting in Mammoth Village, could give no answer, but did offer the next best advice: "Be prepared, and develop an appropriate emergency response plan." One important action urged was to build an emergency access road. One of the two areas identified by the USGS as a likely site of a future erup-

Mammoth Mountain and Mammoth Lakes Village condominiums in Long Valley caldera, eastern Sierra Nevada, California.

tion was the southern rim of Long Valley caldera. The site, near the Casa Diablo Hot Springs geothermal power plant, is just east of the intersection of U.S. 395 and California 203, the only road leading into and out of the village of Mammoth Lakes. Both highways "could well be destroyed by the initial blast," Dan Miller of the USGS warned, "and if that should happen during the wintertime when there is a lot of snow in the encircling mountains, there would be no other way out."

Many residents shifted uncomfortably in their seats at hearing those words and began thinking of an escape route as Miller outlined a possible eruption scenario, based upon one of his less catastrophic sequences:

"An initial steam explosion would throw a devastating wave of extremely hot gases and rock particles that would cut down people, animals, and structures that happen to be in its way, perhaps out to a distance of 12 miles from the vent.

"Ash deposits would build to a foot or more in depth up to 20 miles away.

"Depending on wind and weather conditions at the time of the eruption, several inches of ash could fall on large parts of Nevada, or even in the San Francisco Bay Area to the west.

"But," Miller added, "most eruptions are preceded by days or weeks of precursory events, so I would guess that some warning time might be given local residents to enable them to evacuate the area before a major explosion." It was an unsettling evening.

The first positive result of the meeting was a new sign erected by Inyo National Forest at the nearby hot springs, warning of the dangers at Hot Creek and reminding the public that "12 people have lost their lives in Hot Creek since 1968," with many more seriously injured from such hazards as "scalding water, broken glass, arsenic in the water, sporadic high pollution, sudden temperature changes, unstable ground, and unpredictable eruptions."

"Most people aren't affected by it right now," said Mark Richmond, a local lumber company employee. "It's a point of interest but not a point of concern." Richmond initiated a drive to recall two Mono County supervisors, Michael Jencks and Allen Leydecker, after they voted to declare a state of emergency when the Mono Basin was suddenly hit with a weeklong flurry of small earthquakes. Many in the scientific community were quite alarmed at the time and have since admitted to having wondered if an eruption was really about to happen. One geophysicist conceded, "The thought did cross my mind." Roy Bailey, a USGS geologist then in charge of the agency's volcanic hazards program, voiced the possibility thought of by many "that if the earthquake swarm had gone on with the same intensity as in the first 48 hours, for another few days, we might have done something different." That might have included issuing a volcano watch, the next higher level of hazard warning issued by the USGS for natural disasters. "We all were worried."

Supervisor Jencks said it was possible to group Mammoth Lake people into three categories. "The first group has its head in the sand, like ostriches, and they don't want to know anything about anything. The second group is happy with the emergency planning that's going on, as long as it's all kept behind the scenes. But God help us if we talk about it publicly. The third group is in the minority, but growing, and they welcome candid discussions of the hazard and they're willing to participate in the planning." But Jencks admitted this was the smallest of minorities.

In the small Mammoth community of 4,500 permanent residents, the general attitude a year after the USGS warning was no news is very good news. Most people seemed to prefer not hearing anything about volcanoes or earthquakes. A motel owner concerned about the absence of the usual number of tourists lamented to a *Los Angeles Times* staffer, "If you reporters would just stop writing all this damned volcano stuff, everything would be just fine."

But as much as local civic boosters would like to sweep volcanoes under the rug, they cannot. Even as they tried to evade the subject, swarms of earthquakes continued to be recorded by sensitive seismographs, microshakes that indicated to very concerned investigators measuring every part of the Long Valley that it was time to worry.

Not so the politicians of Mammoth Village. A year after the first warning, a year-round alternate escape route had yet to be built. The proposal to create a county-level office of emergency services was defeated, voted down with little chance the idea would be resurrected. A large segment of the population preferred to deny the reality of a volcanic eruption and the hazard warning and not to seriously concern themselves with the implications to themselves or their families.

Jencks and Leydecker also voted, over the strenuous protests of developers, builders, and building material suppliers, to require an environmental impact statement (EIS) on new construction. Opponents said it would shut down construction in the county and halt growth. Others asked whether writing an EIS about an underground magma chamber would exert as much negative pressure on urban development as the Mammoth Chamber of Commerce exerts political pressure for increased urban development.

An EIS for Mono County was not to be. Mammoth Lakes voted to incorporate, and the recall election of supervisors Leydecker and Jencks was successful, resulting in their removal from county office.

Leydecker, a resident at the time of Mammoth Lakes, had resigned from his longtime civil service position with the United States Forest Service to run for public office, but served only nine months, beginning his term of office on January 3, 1983. He was recalled on November 8 of the same year. When last seen he was on his bicycle leaving town for a cross-country bicycle trip.

A magnitude 5.7 earthquake rattled Round Valley, halfway between Mammoth Lakes and Bishop, in November 1984, and the following string of aftershocks was strong evidence of continuing seismic activity and stirring of underground magma, still quite near the surface, although the magnitudes and frequencies were less than in 1983. This was after an earlier swarm of weak earthquakes—several hundred, three of them stronger than 3—

ruffled the area in July. Scientists thought these small earthquakes were the result of magma melting additional layers of crystalline rock less than four miles below the surface, the intense heat causing rock layers to crack and shake the earth.

Others thought the earthquakes resulted from a crunching together of western basin-and-range valleys and mountains. "When the crust becomes too thin to support its own weight, it fractures and shakes," reports suggested.

"It's a sort of 'chicken and egg' argument," says David Hill, USGS scientist monitoring the Mono Basin. "The two are so closely related you can't really separate them. As the crust thins out and is fractured by earthquakes, the magma rises toward the surface. And as the magma destroys the crust, there are earthquakes."

The scientific debate was of considerable concern to the residents of Owens Valley and Mammoth Lakes. They wanted the federal volcanic hazard warning downgraded. Mer-

chants and townspeople alike tended to blame their economic woes of the past few years on what they repeatedly asserted was a greatly overstated threat of lava movement below the surface of their community.

"The geology hasn't really changed," said Bailey, speaking for the USGS. "We're still dealing with the same problem, a progressing situation."

Local activists knew what the problem was as far as they were concerned—the USGS warning system—and also knew how to make things move in Washington, D.C. Some went over the heads of local scientists and directly to their boss in the Department of the Interior and demanded the rules be changed. "We did everything we could to get responsible statements from the USGS," I was told. The USGS assistant director for engineering geology added, "I'm not saying we didn't get a lot of critical letters from Mammoth people, but that did not sway us."

Nevertheless, the rules were changed by directive from Washington and the old USGS

Geyser Casa Diablo at Southern California Edison geothermal power generating site, Mammoth Lakes, California.

Sierra Nevada crest above Long Valley caldera, John Muir Wilderness, California.

warning system discarded without consulting any of the scientists on the site and directly involved with studies of the Mono Basin. The change was made in the USGS director's office, a high-level decision that did not please many concerned scientists in California who were aware that the new warning procedure would be used against those who regard the situation seriously. The three-level warning system—notice, watch, and warning—was scrapped and replaced by a two-level system—informal alert and formal alert.

Under the new system, the USGS now continues to watch over the magma chambers below Mammoth Lakes and, as long as nothing ominous develops, passes along on an informal basis to local officials and the public the information that nothing has happened.

If something potentially hazardous is noticed that suggests the Long Valley caldera might rupture or the Mono volcanoes explode, well, the USGS will then formally warn people in the affected area to get out.

Real-estate brokers, merchants, and Mayor Gary Flynn wholeheartedly endorsed the new rules and approved of the change. While the status of the volcanic hazard changed only on paper, townspeople claimed the new USGS action to be an actual "downgrading" of the area's volcanic hazard. They felt safer. There was no longer a volcanic hazard warning in Mammoth Lakes.

Sales of condominiums and shopping center rentals quickly improved. A profitable ski season was anticipated and ambitious plans for a new ski bowl near Mammoth's crowded slopes were launched. An 18-hole golf course for summer and fall use was planned, as well as an entirely new high-rise hotel and convention center south of the present resort and on the east rim of the caldera. There was nothing but optimism expressed in the business community following the de-emphasis of the likelihood of volcanic activity. Mayor Flynn echoed the enthusiasm, saying, "Morale has gone up and people feel things are moving ahead."

One troubling decision remained for Mammoth Lakes: how to name and identify the new emergency access road constructed at the urging of USGS scientists by the county and state—an escape hatch if an eruption were to block Highway 203.

The community saw no reason to call attention to the existence of an escape route that would only raise disturbing questions in the minds of visitors about volcanoes and be counterproductive to Mammoth's economic recovery. The euphemism was inspired. The highway marker, in the usual green and white, reads "Mammoth Lakes Scenic Loop."

Eighteen months later, on July 21, 1986, a major earthquake measuring 6.1 on the Richter scale rolled through Mammoth Lakes. It was California's fourth sizable temblor within two weeks, the second strong quake in Mono County in three days, and it rattled the glass of merchant storefronts in Mammoth, shattered plate-glass windows in downtown Bishop, and knocked 53 prefabricated homes from their foundations in nearby Chalfant Valley, destroying some of them completely. The quake was followed in the next few days by over 1,000 aftershocks, including a 5.2 and a 5.1 on an epicenter 15 miles north of Bishop on the edge of the Long Valley caldera. The quake was felt over most of California, in Nevada and Utah, Los Angeles and Salt Lake City.

The expected quake was clearly part of the continuing pattern of seismic activity in the upper Owens Valley and a precursor to even larger quakes. Quakes were already 20 times more numerous in the area than during the previous decade.

From the Menlo Park USGS office came what was described as "an advisory." "It is our assessment that the region of Chalfant Valley, from Bishop north to the Nevada Border, may experience additional earthquakes similar to the July 21 event during the next few days. A less likely larger event, if it occurs, could be felt outside the immediate epicentral region and possibly cause damage in Bishop, Big Pine and north to Mono Lake. We will continue to monitor the situation."

Many residents of Bishop, down the road from Mammoth Lakes, reacted bitterly to the advisory, calling it irresponsible, and said it could scare tourists away from the eastern slopes of the Sierra in the busiest part of the summer season. A fast-food clerk said, "I think they are out to scare us, and they ought to keep their mouths shut."

There was no mention of Mammoth Lakes, located on the edge of the quake epicenter between Bishop and Mono Lake, and no description of the USGS statement as being formal or informal. Apparently, the USGS did not want to be recalled.

Winter skiers still flock to the snow-covered slopes—25,000 and more over crowded weekends. In the summer, hikers and campers stroll on eastern Sierra trails in the shade of yellow pines and fir, cooling their feet in icy streams of melt-water from mini-glaciers high on the Sierra crest. Mammoth Lakes is visited by vacationers whose pleasure on the mountain slopes is not interrupted by earthquake warnings.

They may take a sight-seeing trip to Devils Postpile National Monument to see for themselves what the old lava flow looks like. They would drive, unconcerned, a narrow mountain road with one-way traffic controlled by forest rangers. The visitors may have actually warmed their hands over the steaming fumarole vents above the condominum village and gazed inquistitively into the deep earthquake cracks on the outskirts of town, thinking only what they see and feel was created hundreds—thousands of years ago. Is it reasonable to think that a cataclysmic event creating Long Valley caldera where Mammoth Lakes village is located, could ever occur again—in our lifetime?

Scientists often describe the short living time of human beings on earth, who after all are only visiting, and compare the visit with geological and evolutionary time. Our lives last only a few seconds on the earth's twenty-four hour clock. Much has happened during the evolution of our spinning world, cooling from a molten orb, producing people like us and animals and plant life compatible with twentieth century climate, and a wrinkled landscape as varied as the people of many colors and languages inhabiting it.

Our world continues to evolve and change. In Genesis, we inherit the earth and are destined to subdue it; ostensibly, we want the earth to serve us. Yet, even as we build our cities on the earth, hang ski-lifts from summit ridges, drill into it, bulldoze its surface, convert its irreplaceable minerals into waste and pollution, we, in some respects, change little of the earth by our action. Our bulldozers and dynamite are insignificant compared to the earth's weakest earthquake, smallest lava flow, and lowest tsunami wave. We are still pick-and-shovel laborers compared to the earth's overwhelming natural forces; the shifting of the landscape beneath us, the earthquakes and volcanoes are beyond our control or manipulation. We find it impossible to even imagine the consequences.

We seldom think of our earth as the mostly hot rock it is—a molten, gaseous and radioactive core with a cooling, hard crust—until a thin part on which we live cracks and breaks, and we become aware that our earth has not yet been completed and never will be. It is indeed a fragile place.

Where the landscape is most convoluted it is most noted, written of, and photographed. Where the potential for death and destruction is most ominous is often where we stand in awe. In many ways, we tend to congregate and play where nature's cataclysmic forces are dramatically displayed, because here are the best scenic views from condominums, superior ski runs, unusual landscapes for national parks, and uncovered minerals in upthrusting faults and ancient volcanic rifts. These are the open pages of the earth's geologic history which we seldom deign to respect, for we use the earth as we in turn are threatened by it. Only the timid sell their condos and leave.

Crater Lake, Mt. Rainier, Mt. Lassen, the Grand Tetons, Mammoth Lakes are all geologic masterpieces—landscapes for us to live with and upon if we will only be aware of nature's continuing geologic ferment beneath us. We must always remember the mountain often described in past years as the most gracefully beautiful Cascade peak in the Pacific Northwest, Mt. St. Helens. Its perfect symmetry was often photographed by visitors at Spirit Lake. Mt. St. Helens virtually destroyed itself in a violent convulsion after being quiet for 123 years.

CHAPTER SIX

Volcano Country and Lava Lands

Wizard Island in Crater Lake, Crater Lake National Park, Oregon.

The explosive energy released by Mt. St. Helens can be compared to dropping some 27,000 Hiroshima-sized atomic bombs at the rate of nearly one per second for nine hours—that is about 100 times the generating capacity of all United States electric-power stations combined.

Mt. St. Helens had been quiet for over 100 years, but because of a careful study of seismic instruments scattered around the snow-covered peak, United States Geological Survey (USGS) scientists were able to predict renewed eruption activity within a few days. Swarms of harmonic tremors had revealed movement of magma beneath the summit.

Only a few days error in 100 years may be considered close enough, but volcanologists were unable to predict in a positive manner the precise time and place. "Somewhere on the north side of the mountain" was hardly sufficient for local residents and lumbermen. Scientists have not yet solved the ancient problem of how sure we must be before crying wolf, experience acquired at St. Helens notwithstanding. Intensive observations and sophisticated instrumental monitoring have only demonstrated it will be some time before we can actually know where and when.

Scientists had concluded 25 years ago that St. Helens was a bad character, even though it was last active with many eruptions between 1831 and 1857, at a time when few white settlers were around to catalog its performance. Among many names they gave the mountain, Loowit seems most appropriate. It translates Lady of Fire.

In a 1978 report, geologists Dwight Crandell and Donald Mullineaux wrote of St. Helens's record: "Over the preceding 4,500 years the mountain erupted more often and more violently than any other volcano in the contiguous 48 states. Over the years it has produced lava domes too viscous to do anything more than grow into dangerous plugs,

large quantities of volcanic ash and pumice falling over an area of thousands of square miles, destructive mud flows of hot ash, lava flows, and massive mud flows filling stream valleys draining the mountain slopes." The average number of years between eruptions was 225. St. Helens was ahead of schedule when it finally did let go, as expected by Crandell and Mullineaux.

"In the future, Mt. St. Helens probably will erupt violently and intermittently, just as it has in the recent geologic past," they forecast. "These future eruptions will affect human life and health, property, agriculture and general economic welfare over a broad area. The volcano's behavior pattern suggests that the current quiet interval will not last as long as 1,000 years; instead an eruption is more likely to occur within the next 100 years, and perhaps even before the end of this century."

After hearing reports that mountain roads around St. Helens "looked like downtown Seattle at rush hour," the governor ordered approaches to the shaking, fuming mountain blockaded to keep away the curious. As potential danger of violent eruptions became increasingly apparent, residents were urged to leave the area immediately. Many did not.

At 7:00 A.M. Pacific Daylight Time on May 18, 1980, geologists Dorothy and Keith Stoffel took off in their light plane from Yakima Airport to reconnoiter the mountain and photograph its steaming hulk. They made several circuits around and over the summit area without seeing any activity, other than huge cracks opening in the snow as the mountain swelled from internal pressure. At 8:32 A.M. the mountain shook from a 5.1 magnitude quake centered below the north flank at the very moment the Stoffels were looking directly down onto the summit.

"The whole north side of the summit crater began to move instantaneously as one gigantic mass," recalled Dorothy Stoffel, as reported in *Scientific American*. "The entire

Windy Ridge, Mt. St. Helens National Monument, Washington.

Summit crater, Mt. St. Helens National Monument, Washington.

mass began to ripple and churn without moving laterally. Then the whole north side of the summit started moving to the north. . . ." Seconds later the mountain exploded. Taking a last photo, they dived to the south in the plane at full throttle to escape the rapidly expanding cloud of hot ash. They landed safely in Portland as giant ash clouds boiled upward in billowing mushroom shapes, lighted internally by lightning bolts that were part of a steam blast and magma explosion. The blast moved outward—an expanding wall of debris—at speeds of an estimated 500 miles an hour. No one within the blast area escaped alive, and a forest was destroyed.

THE EXPLOSIVE ERUPTION of Mt. St. Helens, one of the 15 major volcanoes in the Cascade Range extending from Mt. Lassen in north-

ern California to Mt. Garibaldi in British Columbia across the Canadian border, is a reminder that the Pacific Northwest landscape, covered with ancient lava flows and pimpled with volcanic peaks, is geologically alive and subject to considerable change at any time. Pushed and shoved by the Juan de Fuca plate, an eastern section of the giant Pacific Ocean plate pushing beneath the continent, the mountainous Northwest is another example of continental wanderlust.

Where the San Andreas fault slips beneath the ocean off Cape Mendocino in northern California, the dense and heavier Pacific plate no longer slides against the lighter mass of the North American plate moving westward but dives beneath into a region below the earth's surface. High temperatures and pressure some 60 to 125 miles below the surface cause rock to soften and form magma, molten rock that upon reaching the surface becomes lava.

What actually happens as one plate slides beneath the other is still debated among scientists who are aware that this is one area in which our knowledge is the least advanced. It is suspected that magma is produced between the diving plate and the lower mantle, but in the complicated environment beneath the earth's crust, a variety of unknown phenomena is operating, including high temperatures, changes in pressure, water intrusion—all may be acting to melt the softened rock—or it may simply be that movement of the plates encounters a weak part of the crust and forces the transfer of existing magma toward the surface. Minerals coalesce with the molten material, and because they are more buoyant than surrounding solidified rock, the magma slowly percolates upward, like bubbles rising in a jar of honey. Magma eventually accumulates in pockets located from about two miles to several miles beneath the surface. If the magma is very liquid and gases gradually escape, the magma chamber may remain in place for a considerable period of time before disturbances on the surface weaken the crust and allow the magma plume to break out.

Some erupt explosively, such as Mt. Lassen and Mt. St. Helens, volcanoes with magma composed largely of a mix of silica compounds, water vapor, and various gases trapped within the viscous molten material until it nears the surface. Under such circumstances pressure is released and the gases escape explosively, often carrying with them parts of the mountain broken into fragments as fine as powder. These particles may be carried long distances by the wind until they fall to the earth as ash. When glowing debris quickly melts the ice and snow on high mountain slopes, torrents of scalding water and superheated incandescent gas, steam, and ash blow down into adjacent valleys, combining with other materials accumulated on the way and changing into a hot mud flow moving at rapid speeds, obliterating everything in its path. From Mt. St. Helens a mud flow poured down the Toutle River Valley reaching the Columbia River, a hundred miles downstream from the erupting vent. In prehistoric times mud flows raced down the sides of Mt. Rainier, traveling as far as 50 miles in minutes. Mud flows are a particularly dangerous aspect of active, snow-capped volcanic peaks, for residents don't expect to be affected so many miles from the eruption

and there's little time to warn them.

An important goal of volcanologists is being able to warn people about possible movements in shifting plates that result in earthquakes and volcanic eruptions, but predicting what the geological earth will do at present is little more than a technological hodgepodge of instrumental readings, empirical evidence, reading of historical cycles, common sense, and luck. As with earthquakes, geologists can often say an eruption will occur, but can only give an

Mt. St. Helens, May 18, 1980. U.S. Geological Survey photo.

Geothermal power development, Geysers, California.

extended estimate of when. Unless seismic measurements give them some idea of exactly where, they will be able to say very little about how big. Over the long range, scientists using knowledge of historical events, radiometric dating of lava flows and ash falls, and readings of tree-ring aberrations in mud-flow valleys can often reconstruct the history of a volcanic region and make long-range predictions, even when they sometimes appear more like guesses than the result of careful scientific evaluation. Mark Twain commented wryly on these procedures when he wrote, "There is something fascinating about science. One gets such wholesale returns of conjecture out of such a trifling investment of fact." But then, it is quite evident that knowledge of a volcano's misbehavior in past centuries could well provide an accurate indication of dangerous activity in the future, making a knowledgeable prediction important to the public, even when

an announced prediction that is wrong could cost an urban economy billions of dollars.

Cautious scientists remember with a wince their premature warning ten years ago that Soufrière volcano on the Caribbean island of Guadeloupe would erupt violently when it began spouting a heavy ash plume. Geologists' alarms indicating a possible eruption—similar to the blast occurring on Martinique in 1902 when 30,000 people were killed—goaded authorities into evacuating more than 70,000 people from their island homes and businesses, keeping them away for 3½ months. Except for a little smoke and ash, nothing happened.

Short-term divination calls for assembling a multitude of clues through observation and measurement: seismic activity that may be barely felt; emission of puffs of ash and gas; and appearance of cracks in the ice on high mountain glaciers. Harmonic vibrations and rumblings that indicate below-surface movement of lava and opening of cracks almost always precede an eruption, continuing for hours until magma reaches the surface or gases breach the vent. Here tiltmeters and laser ranging devices are used to measure swelling of the volcanic cone caused by magma oozing upward and nearing the surface.

With such evidence to consider, scientists have targeted several potential volcanic sites along the edge of the continental plate as candidates for careful watching—they may erupt in the near future. Of particular concern to volcanologists are many Cascade peaks and areas of geologically unstable crust covering the subducting Juan de Fuca plate. Among the volcanic areas that have been building up over the last two million years, some erupting in recent times, are these:

The Mono Basin-Long Valley Caldera at Mammoth Lakes Resort, California

The area between Clear Lake and the geysers in northern California

Mt. Shasta and nearby Medicine Lake Highlands, California

Mt. Lassen, California, last erupted in 1915

Crater Lake, Oregon

The Three Sisters, Oregon

Mt. Hood, Oregon

Mt. St. Helens, Washington, last erupted in 1980

Mt. Rainier, Washington

Mt. Baker, Washington

Glacier Peak, Washington, last erupted about 1650

Mt. St. Augustine, Alaska, last erupted in 1986

The potential effect of the subducting Pacific plate extends over an area far beyond the obvious chain of Cascade peaks into regions of the west where scientists are missing geological information that would enable them to definitely determine where the influence of overlapping plates below will be most felt by people above. There is disagreement on how far south in California the Pacific plate may be pushing magma to the surface, but magma movement in the Mono Lake area appears to be a direct result

of the same plate shifting that forced the eruption of Mt. St. Helens and even now may be heating up the crust far beneath Mt. Shasta. Under the Pacific Ocean about 270 miles off the Oregon coast, geologists have discovered an undersea volcano spewing rich deposits of minerals and sulfides in an area where the Juan de Fuca plate begins its dip beneath the continent.

The states of Oregon and Washington, covering most of the area along this dipping

Multnomah Falls with lava flows exposed, Columbia River Gorge, Oregon.

Ancient ash deposits and lava flows, Smith Rock State Park, Oregon.

and has been sliding beneath the continental plate at a speed of about one inch per year. At present it slips quietly under the larger plate without fracturing in large tremblors, or perhaps it is temporarily blocked as occasionally also happens with the horizontally sliding San Andreas fault. This situation could change at any time with the possibility of a large earthquake or new volcanic eruption. Scientists simply do not know what is happening so far beneath the earth's surface.

The most accurate information being gathered that could be used in interpreting deformation and drift of the earth is kept secret by the Pentagon. The Air Force's NAV-STAR satellites can determine precise locations on the earth within an inch and are designed mainly to help guide missiles to their targets. This extraordinarily accurate information from satellites orbiting the earth is withheld on security grounds. Secrecy is also clamped on information obtained from the Navy's GEOSAT system, which maps the shape of the ocean floor based on gravitational irregularities in the sea surface. Geophysicists trying to study historical patterns revealed in the planetary crust have nothing available to them that matches the detail of the naval charts, but such maps are classified information.

Apart from trying to interpret information from a multitude of new technological sources, it isn't easy to find out something new when the source is an apparent gap in information, a place where nothing has happened. Such a location is the Aleutian Islands, where four of the most powerful earthquakes in recent history have occurred along the chain of active volcanic islands, with a notable exception at the eastern end, the Shumagin Islands where there has never been a great earthquake recorded. The Shumagins are a seismic gap, a place of ominous quiet surrounded by islands where many earthquakes have been measured in recent years, a place where scientists conclude that stresses must be building and about to let go. Concern over future quakes where none has occurred before has its counterpart in the concern over nuclear power plants and nuclear storage sites located in volcanic areas where they would in all probability never have been built if Mt. St. Helens had erupted 40 years sooner.

One of the nation's largest nuclear power plants, Oregon's Trojan facility, located on

oceanic plate, have never been shaken by a giant earthquake in historic times, yet the crusted slabs overlying each other could produce shocks as strong as any felt in California or Alaska. The worst earthquake recorded in the Northwest occurred in 1949 and measured a Richter 7. The 1964 Alaska quake was 8.5.

The Juan de Fuca plate is relatively young, perhaps only ten to fifteen million years old. It is a section of the much larger Pacific plate the Columbia River just 33 miles from Mt. St. Helens, was reevaluated by the Nuclear Regulatory Commission's (NRC) Geosciences Division after Mt. St. Helens's violent eruption. Nothing was felt at the plant site and only a thin layer of volcanic ash dusted the plant. Little more than a "severe dust storm," reported the plant manager. "I don't think that mountain is capable of doing anything to hurt the plant."

NRC licensing project manager C. M. Trammell was more cautious, asking, "Did we do it right when we licensed the plant or should we take another look at it because of the volcano?" The Trojan plant began producing power in 1976, and possible volcanic activity was considered by the NRC when an operating license was first granted. While not ruling out an eruption at Mt. St. Helens—an event not seriously considered—NRC scientists concluded in 1978 that "there is no present increase in volcanic activity in the Cascade volcanoes. The historic record

shows that Mt. St. Helens was far more active during the 19th century than during the 20th century." Apparently NRC scientists were not speaking to USGS people when in 1978 they predicted that Mt. St. Helens would erupt again.

People living in volcano country, even at the foot of major volcanic peaks, seldom worry about possible eruptions that may or may not ever occur. The attitude is one of being aware a mountain may blow its top but that it might not happen for 500 years. "We can't stop living and it's a waste of time worrying about it," is often repeated. Yet the volcanoes of the Cascades and the great Columbia plateau are the site of what have been among the most violent events in earth's recent history, and some of them will certainly recur. All 18 Cascade volcanoes, from Mt. Baker near the Canadian border south to Mt. Lassen in California, began forming about two million years ago and probably reached their present height 700,000 or fewer years

South Sister, Cascade Range near Bend, Oregon.

Broken Top, Cascade Range, Oregon.

ago. It was only about 7,000 years ago that Mt. Mazama, which may have been one of the highest Cascade peaks, erupted in a gigantic explosion incinerating most of the volcano into ash. Remnants of the cone then collapsed into the empty magma chamber beneath. Crater Lake is all that remains.

Many geologists believe that another Cascade peak may also explode on a scale comparable to the Mazama cataclysm. It would be an awesome event. Grant Heiken, a specialist in volcanism at the Los Alamos Scientific Laboratory, has observed, "A safe distance from which to watch the event might be the earth's orbit of a space station."

Destructive earthquakes in the Pacific Northwest can be considered remote, unless the Pacific plate begins to move in sudden jerks as it slides beneath the continental plate, shaking the crustal landscape above. Dormant volcanoes would awaken, new breaks in weak sections of the earth might erupt into volcanic peaks, but any earthquakes would be mostly quite local and not felt much beyond volcanic epicenters.

Potential hazards from future eruptions are quite real, however, as Mt. St. Helens demonstrated in its 1980 eruption. A simple change in wind direction would have partially buried the northwest's second largest urban region and the city of Portland in hot ash a foot deep, temporarily crippling the city and Columbia River commerce.

Within a year of Mt. St. Helens's eruption, USGS warnings were issued advising of the possibility of Mt. Hood erupting. Seismographs had recorded minor earthquakes indicating that the Cascade peak may be stirring again after some 200 to 300 years of silence, although relatively insignificant disturbances may have occurred as recently as 1859 and 1865, when an observer described the top of Mt. Hood as being "enveloped in smoke and flame."

Published reports by the USGS have diagramed possible destruction from potential ash fallout, mud flows, floods, lateral blasts from the summit, and flowing earthslides of rock fragments ejected from the volcano. Most damage would be in the immediate area of the south slopes of Mt. Hood, where Timberline Lodge and the government camp area below would most certainly be destroyed. Again, depending on wind direction, ash fallout would seriously damage crops in the Hood River Valley and mud flows could fill the East Fork Hood River channel. Mud flows and floods would also sweep down the Sandy and Zigzag River valleys to Brightwood and beyond, possibly reaching the Columbia River at Troutdale. Floodplains along the Sandy River could be buried in as much as 45 feet of mud and flood water, should the eruption occur in winter months. With winds flowing westerly toward Portland, the city would be forced to shut down in the ash fallout and automobile traffic would be slowed as in a major snowfall. No lava flows have occurred since the last glacier retreated off the mountain and there is little reason to believe they will occur again in the foreseeable future, but by all evidence, molten rock is still present within Mt. Hood.

Anyone who has struggled to the icy twin summit craters on Mt. Rainier is well aware that this highest peak in the northwest is still hot inside. Rainier's rim rocks are kept snow-free all year by heat and steam from within the mountain which last erupted perhaps 100 years ago. Today the many-glaciered peak is quiet, but the giant volcano continues to produce occasional steam explosions and rock slides where subsurface glacier heating has occurred. They are signs of geologic restlessness, sufficient for scientists to keep a close volcanic watch over the mountain. Earthquake monitoring stations record swarms of harmonic vibrations indicating that magma in the mountain's interior may be rising toward the surface.

Sproat Lake in coastal volcanic range, Vancouver Island, British Columbia, Canada.

Aircraft chartered by the USGS regularly fly over the mountain on infrared monitoring surveys measuring changes in temperature of steam vents and areas of hot rock. Volcanic activity continues within Mt. Rainier's subterranean magma chamber.

Mt. Rainier will surely erupt again some time within the next few hundred years, according to USGS investigations, but like other volcanoes in the Cascades and earthquakes in California, at present there is no way to predict when. Over the short term, warnings are possible when measurements detect internal stresses and rapid movement of magma, but as Mt. St. Helens demonstrated, the potential awesome destructiveness of Mt. Rainier will not be known until it actually erupts in a major Washington state disaster.

A cataclysmic explosion like that of Mt. Mazama is considered highly unlikely, at least within the next few centuries. But a less violent eruption would still cause serious hazards such as mud flows moving down valley floors and covering floodplains, along with ash fallout over many hundreds of square miles downwind. Rock avalanches would probably bury valleys within a few miles of the base of Mt. Rainier and serious flooding would occur in river basins as far distant as Tacoma.

Based on what has happened during the past 7,000 years and may well happen again, USGS scientist Dwight Crandell predicts possible ash fallout reaching 30 miles downwind totalling not more than an inch or so. Only in the immediate flank area of Mt. Rainier would there be a high degree of danger to human life from asphyxiation, falling rock fragments, and ash accumulation. Travelers on Chinook Pass highways could expect to be battered by falling rocks and considerable ash, if they had not heeded warnings to stay out of the area.

Mud flows would fill the Nisqually River valley as far as Alder Lake, the White River to Mud Mountain Dam, and the Puyallup all the way to Sumner, with some flooding possibly reaching Puget Sound and the flat valley beyond Algona. Historic wind data suggests there is little chance of hot ash erupting from Mt. Rainier ever falling in Seattle or Tacoma, and any lava flows would be restricted to summit flanks, but visitors and residents of Seattle and Tacoma will experience what may be the most spectacular volcanic display to ever occur in a populated area. Tourist promotion people will love it.

Lost Lake and Newberry Crater lava flow, Oregon.

THE LANDSCAPE from the Oregon coast inland to Yellowstone is littered with volcanoes, ancient cinder cones, giant rift cracks, thousands of square miles of lava flows, and many hot springs and underground thermal water sources. Within a few miles of now quiet vol-

Mt. Hood reflected in Timothy Lake, Cascade Range, Oregon, South of the Columbia River Gorge.

canic vents in Craters of the Moon National Monument, atop lava flows covering the nation's most extensive aquifer, is the Idaho National Engineering Laboratory (INEL), with 52 nuclear reactors, 17 operational, the largest concentration of reactors in the world. It is here that Idaho's Lost River flows beneath ancient lava flows to reappear over a hundred miles south, cascading into the Snake River at Twin Falls.

Originally established in 1949 as the National Reactor Testing Station during the days when government facilities were given names clearly identifying their purpose, the INEL, as the installation is locally known, brought an economic boom to south central Idaho. When the government announced its plan to build the first operating nuclear reactor on the site, according to a resident at nearby Arco, people "danced in the streets." There was no discernible opposition. In those days, the development of nuclear energy was

viewed as a boon to mankind. A large sign at the highway intersection with Arco's main street still proudly boasts of Arco being the first city in the nation lighted by nuclear power.

Today, INEL is one of the largest employers in the state and enjoys considerable clout with state legislators, but if an environmental impact statement had been prepared prior to construction using geologic information available today, it is questionable whether INEL would have been built. INEL is located in a geologically unstable region rated by the USGS as Seismic Zone 3, the same earthquake zone rating as San Francisco. An earthquake could dump enormous quantities of stored nuclear waste into the Snake River aquifer.

Exhausted nuclear fuel rods removed from reactors aboard nuclear submarines, aircraft carriers, and power plants may possibly be the most dangerous material produced by

Plutonium 239 is capable, in extremely minute quantities, of giving off highly lethal alpha particles. With a decay half-life of many thousands of years, it requires permanent storage without any possibility of human contamination for hundreds of thousands to millions of years. At the INEL Exxon radio-active-waste processing and storage plant, I stared with considerable respect at the spent rods standing deep in their concrete storage pool, silently emitting a deep blue, deadly glow. INEL is currently storing over seven million cubic feet of nuclear waste, including 1200 pounds of plutonium.

Seepage of radiation has already occurred through the underlying basaltic lava. USGS staff have found traces of plutonium nearly halfway into the aquifer at 240 feet below the surface. Tons of nonradioactive but highly toxic materials have also been injected into the aquifer and Iodine 129 has been found 2½ miles from the reprocessing plant.

Should the Snake River aquifer become seriously contaminated by radioactive wastes stored at INEL and released by earthquake or volcanic activity—a distinct possibility—the consequences would be devastating to the many hundreds of farms and communities in southern Idaho; indeed a threat is posed to the entire Columbia River basin.

Some kind of volcanism has always been part of the west. It is the stuff of which scenery is made, the west of national parks and landscapes in a variety unknown elsewhere in the nation. Volcanoes offer a mix of dramatic beauty, dreadful delight, and a kind of pleasurable foreboding, and they have not been wholly destructive—their widespread ash deposits have enriched the land of every western state, and the high peaks have generated weather conducive to a good life and the water and power necessary for irrigating farmlands and recreation. Volcanoes will always be beckoning like the feathered serpent of antiquity—brilliant and deadly.

Castle Geyser, Upper Geyser Basin, Yellowstone National Park, Wyoming.

modern society. Of the spent fuel, 98 percent is radionuclides that effectively decompose in 150 days. But the remaining 2 percent, recovered during waste processing by private operators at INEL, is composed of the most deadly matter known, plutonium 239. It is a cancer inducer far worse than comparable nonradioactive pollutants such as lead, arsenic, and cadmium. Iodine 129, with a half-life of 16.4 million years, is also present.

ACROSS THE FLATLANDS of eastern Oregon, northern California, and southern Idaho, are the western lava lands, a prairie of lava so geologically recent the black rock has not yet decomposed into dirt. In some areas the cold lava is smooth, ropy-textured pahoe-hoe; in other places, the rough impossible-to-walk-on aa is more prevalent. From the air the black landscape, softened in part by forest, extends for thousands of square miles, a terrain with few towns, farms, or roads.

The lava issued from vents forced open by magma rising from the subducting oceanic plate. Inland from the larger vents that produce high volcanic peaks in the Cascades— as if the powerful forces necessary for volcanic eruptions were mostly spent in producing mountains like the Three Sisters, Mazama, and Shasta—smaller amounts of magma were able to build immature cinder and spatter cones.

South of Bend, Oregon, at Fort Rock State Park, the low fort-like formation called a tuff-ring rises only 300 feet above the barren volcanic desert. It was formed when magma rising to the surface came in contact with ground water; the eruptive reaction threw volcanic debris and ash in a circular pattern around the vent, forming a ring-like rock wall.

Nearby, a similar column of magma also contacted the underground water source and exploded violently, creating an immense circular pit 450 feet deep and a mile in diameter. Forest Service maps identify that opening in the earth as "Hole-in-the-Ground", so named by early residents. The highest cinder cone in the area, Lava Butte, is only as wide and as high as the hole. Both were formed about 6,000 years ago.

Below the Oregon border in northern California is Lava Beds National Monument at Tule Lake, where magma was forced to the surface through a cluster of vents. Great masses of basaltic lava spread over the surrounding area, forming a rugged landscape mostly of pahoehoe that surrounds the bases of cinder cone buttes. Covering the lava in many areas are remnants of ash fallout from large volcanic eruptions. This cover is the same material that buried Teotihuacan in Mexico and Pompeii and Herculaneum in the Roman Empire.

The apparent flatness of the Tule Lake region is deceiving to the casual observer, for the landscape hides uncounted layers of ancient lava flows—some 30,000 years old— built one atop the other. This complex, when measured from its depths, may contain fifty times the bulk of Mt. Shasta, the dormant volcano easily seen in the west.

The most recent eruptions in the area occurred about a thousand years ago. The lava formed a network of caves and tubes, and hot, highly fluid lava ran through them like a brook. When eruptions ceased, the lava drained to lower levels, ultimately leaving open tubes, many large enough for visitors to walk or crawl in. All offer a fascinating journey through tunnels named Devils Playground by an early settler. Local Modoc Indians said of the area, "You are standing at the center of the world," and the primeval landscape does bring to mind the earth's hot and violent beginnings.

Geologists consider the area still potentially active, and nineteenth century Modoc Indians in the region of Tule Lake and Shasta may have been aware they lived in the shadow of violence when, after disputes with local settlers, they took refuge within the lava beds. In 1872 the small Modoc band held out against superior numbers of U.S. Army troops for almost six months, frustrating again and again the attempts of soldiers and volunteers not familiar with the area to find them in the maze of passageways, tubes, and caves of lava. It became a major Indian war, the only one fought in California. As the volcanic lava extrusions gave the Modoc a last chance, the nearness of death surely exalted life. The fields of lava were an intimate companion of hope and destruction.

CHAPTER SEVEN

Creating Parks and Controversy

Grand Prismatic Springs, Midway Geyser Basin, Yellowstone National Park, Wyoming.

It all happened after the formation of the earth about 4,500 million years ago, long after the original, single land mass broke up and recognizable continental shapes began drifting and sliding toward their present location. The North American continental plate drifted westward, in places covered by ocean waters 6 miles deep, until the flat plate encountered the Pacific plate sliding northwest. The collision caused the heavier oceanic plate to slide under the continental plate until about 100 million years ago along what is now the California coast. This forced the lighter continental rocks to heave upward above sea level, warping and breaking the crust into mountain ranges and basins.

Scoured by glaciers and eroded by rivers in subsequent eras, the process has slowed in recent centuries, but earthquakes and volcanoes, hot springs and geysers remain as evidence of continents continuing to drift, of valleys sinking, and mountain ranges still thrusting upward. Along the northern California and Pacific Northwest coasts, the oceanic plate continues to slip beneath the continent, breaking the crust and allowing magma to release its energy in explosive volcanoes.

The mountains in the western United States—the great ranges known as the Sierra and Cascades, the Bitterroot and Wasatch, and the Rocky Mountains that divide the continent between east and west—rose about 60 million years ago and are young by geologic measure. The oldest exposed rocks in the west are about 2.5 billion years old. These rocks can be seen and touched in the bottom of the Grand Canyon of the Colorado and represent the beginnings of the North American continent.

FLORA AND FAUNA are popular subjects for graphic artists and photographers, but mountain landscapes may be the prime theme of most photographers. From the very earliest days when cumbersome cameras and slow film emulsions caused mountains to be favored subjects because they don't move to the tourists of today with Instamatics who are merely awed, the wrinkled crust of upthrust mountain ranges, volcanic peaks, and faulted valleys remains an inspiration to even the most jaded visitor of the outdoor west.

Mountains and valleys, the geological consequences of drifting continents eroded and polished by rivers and glaciers, are glorified as places of scenic grandeur and inspiration to the human spirit. To the tourist-photographer and the professional with a view camera, the challenges of portraying a complex wilderness world are demanding and satisfying. In the case of our first national park, Yellowstone, paintings and photographs of the unique thermal features by William Jackson and Thomas Moran were undoubtedly instrumental in convincing Congress that Yellowstone country should be protected and preserved for future generations.

The evolutionary upright-walking people that began populating the earth assuredly never thought it was going to be necessary to draw lines around a geological disturbance to preserve and protect the rocks, but people, whose presence represents the minutest fraction of geologic time, when advised to "populate and subdue" the earth have found it quite difficult to preserve the earth. It was not until after nations and rule by law evolved that an appreciation of wildness and the beauty of the earth developed along with a philosophy to protect the natural world from the people who live on it.

The national park system exists in part because the spectacularly beautiful mountains and valleys, volcanic craters and peaks, geysers and hot springs—all primordial evidence of continental beginnings—demanded

Mt. Rainier and White River, Mt. Rainier National Park, Washington.

preservation. They inspired the idealism that fostered the concept of national parks, preserves of primitive scenery and mountain skylines that exert a powerful influence in shaping our character and responses to each other. We understand that the earth is our greatest heritage. We are, as Robinson Jeffers so eloquently expressed, "not man apart."

Artists with brush or film know this relationship well and share their experience with us. The windblown sand, cloudless desert sky, and weathered rock are the sensuous personal vision of Georgia O'Keeffe. The Atlantic coast becomes almost unrecognizable subjective images when interpreted by John Marin. Northeastern coastal scenes become primitive again when touched by Rockwell Kent; Ansel Adams's photographs of Yosemite reveal shapes and moods we never saw before; Edward Weston gives us tidepools to look into for a glimpse of the inner world; and Ernest Braun tries to take us inside rocks and beyond what we see with our own eyes. Perhaps by representing them in a subjective manner we are trying to reclaim, if only for a moment on the printed page, some earlier times.

Ansel Adams wrote, "Here are worlds of experience beyond the world of aggressive man, beyond history, beyond science. The moods and qualities of nature and the relations of great art are equally difficult to define; we can grasp them only in the depths of our perceptive spirit."

The national park system, monuments, and many no less important state parks preserve the untamed ecosystems of our changing earth and afford opportunities to appreciate the dramatic landforms and associated wildlife. They represent a unique vision of the earth, possibly a subliminal recognition of all that has gone on before, a symbol of stability in a changing world, and a standard of beauty.

Cinder cones and lava flow, Sunset Crater National Monument, Arizona.

An unexpected appreciation of our need for an untrammeled environment occurred during an after-dinner meeting at the White House with President Lyndon Johnson and environmental activists visiting from around the nation. President Johnson had that same day ordered U.S. Marines into the Dominican Republic "to preserve order," as the afternoon newspapers explained. The president, in commenting on his military order, said, "I sent troops to the Dominican Republic this morning, but the most important thing I've done today is meet with you and talk about a beautiful America. After all, this is what it's all about."

I was reminded of an event 100 years earlier when, during the darkest days of America's history, thousands were dying on Civil War battlefields and President Lincoln thought it important to step away from war long enough to sign an Act of Congress to set aside for "public use and enjoyment the valley of Yosemite." The Civil War was not yet over, but the preservation of the valley and giant sequoias of Yosemite was undoubtedly looked upon as a patriotic issue—affirmation that the nation would prevail and Yosemite would be preserved for future generations. The seeds of a national park system had been planted. They would germinate amid the geysers and hot springs of Yellowstone.

It was no coincidence that the national park system began in the west, where dramatic convoluted landscapes echoed the origin of the earth, inspiring every traveler headed west aboard the new railroads. The frontier west possessed not only the raw resources for a new life—even gold in the hills—but also stimulating symbols on a grand scale to invoke a successful rendezvous with the future.

Basin-and-range country offered inviting valleys to settle in and challenging mountain ranges to go beyond. It was like nothing anywhere on the eastern seaboard, and with such articulate early travelers as Frederick Olmstead and John Muir to describe the giant trees and granite monoliths of such unique discoveries as Yosemite, the idealism of preservation assumed its own life.

WHILE ALL NATIONAL PARKS established over the years in one way or another exhibit in dramatic fashion the geologic performance of the continent in progress, some parks display their geological beginnings more obviously than others. It is these parks and monuments that reveal how a drifting continent and volcanoes created the western landscape. Geologic disruptions of the land also provide special opportunities for commercial exploitation, and when not reserved exclusively for public use with natural amenities preserved by law, degradation can be complete. As the behavior of people may be adversely affected by the discovery of gold, so can hot springs change a life or even the location of a town. Thermopolis is an excellent example.

Hot springs are common geologic events all over the west, one guidebook listing hundreds, and many unlisted are hardly more than individual bath tubs. Arkansas Hot Springs National Park is the most renowned hot spring complex, but in northwestern Wyoming, where the continent drifts over a deep crack in the earth's mantle over a "hot spot," as geologists call it, is the not so well known Thermopolis Hot Springs State Park, site of the largest hot mineral springs in the world. It produces over 16 million gallons of 135° Fahrenheit water every 24 hours. Twenty-seven different minerals are present in the water, mostly sodium, bicarbonate, sulfate, and chloride.

Known to the local Shoshone Indians as *Bah-gue-wana*, or smoking waters, the hot springs must have been of considerable religious significance as the Indians were convinced the water came from deep within the earth and brought to the surface health-giving elements. The warmth of the water meant to the Shoshones that it issued from the "heart

Grand Teton, Grand Teton National Park, Wyoming.

of the world" as did the blood from the heart of a bison. Early white settlers in the area recognized the health benefits to be derived from bathing in the mineral waters, even considered the hot water not unpleasant to drink, "and with salt and pepper added tasted very much like chicken soup." A drink was considered good for colic.

The subsurface geology of Thermopolis quietly bubbling from a clear pool at the base of a limestone cliff is very different from Yellowstone's underground piping generating powerful geysers. Thermopolis's water enters underground limestone strata high in the Owl Creek Mountains several miles distant and flows downward through aquifers where the water is heated from rocks deep beneath the surface. At the Big Horn River a major fault interrupts the water's flow underground and the mineral-laden water, carrying dissolved chemicals picked up along the way, reaches the surface and spreads out in broad travertine terraces at the river's edge.

Wyoming politicians and federal Indian commissioners believed the hot springs could become world famous if improvements were made to make them more accessible to travelers. Negotiations were begun with the Arapahoe and Shoshone Indians; the springs are located on the Wind River Reservation occupied by both tribes. The federal government offered $60,000 for 100 square miles of Indian lands including the hot springs, and the Indians accepted in an elaborate treaty-signing ceremony, now celebrated every summer at Thermopolis in a colorful pageant named "The Gift of the Waters." Considering the bargain price paid, mostly in cattle, bacon, sugar, and coffee, with the Indians retaining only the right to camp and bathe at the springs, it was indeed a gift. Shoshone Chief Washakie said at the treaty signing in 1896, "I have given you the springs. My heart feels good."

By various means over the years the idealistic intentions so solemnly agreed to with the Indians were compromised by white settlers. Most of the land purchased eventually became the incorporated city of Thermopolis, moved lock, stock, and barrel from its

Thermopolis Hot Springs limestone cascades on the Big Horn River, Thermopolis, Wyoming.

original townsite at Owl Creek to take advantage of the potential commercial opportunities of the remaining acreage along the Big Horn River. Only a few acres were reserved as open space for camping by visitors and Indians and for free bathing in hot spring waters.

Most townspeople fully supported commercial use of the land; "sites for bathing houses, hospitals, and sanitariums should be leased"; but they added, "The state should retain absolute control of a quantity of water sufficient to furnish baths free of charge . . . and erect and maintain a free bathing house with modest apartments. . . ." Newspapers in the state supported free baths and free camping, agreeing that a "pauper's pledge should not have to be given in order to obtain the baths." The press commented at length on the dangers of leasing the hot springs for what would become an exclusive privilege, and reminded those who would listen how the hot springs "have almost been offered free for the public by the generous Indians." If the state leased the springs the object of the transfer would be lost. The results of the debate, held in the climate of a frontier west, could have been easily predicted.

In the summer of 1897, Chief Washakie of the Shoshones, feeble and in poor health, completely paralyzed on one side, arrived on one of the last visits to his springs. Bathing in the hot mineral water so improved the physical condition of the old warrior that he recovered much of his former vigor and lived for another three years. But Chief Washakie lived to see the hot springs public areas steadily diminish, as individuals erected increasing numbers of private bathhouses on state property around the terrace pools. The editor of the local newspaper complained in every edition about the illegal squatters and lack of maintenance, spearheading a campaign to maintain free camping and bathing privileges. It was possibly in part the frustration over what was happening to the hot springs that sent the editor to the state insane asylum.

In their book *Ghost Towns of Wyoming*, Mary Lou Pence and Lola Homsher wrote indignantly that ". . . the state legislature . . . granted the old chieftain's wishes. He was given one of the springs. The right of a lot of others to wash in it was granted, too. It is the one designated 'for public use.' A shameful gift, hardly deserving its present poetic name, 'Gift of the Waters!' " Chief Washakie

clearly wanted the hot springs to be set aside "for the free use of all men of all races, creeds and colors forever," but nothing of the kind was included in the treaty. The intelligent but illiterate old chief was deceived.

Thermopolis Hot Springs was the jet set resort of the 1890s, the Saratoga Springs of the west. The travertine falls that drop into the Big Horn River became Lovers' Leap. There were few trees and grassy lawns, but there was a dance pavilion, bars, gambling, and hotels. Indians were welcomed as distinguished guests, others greeted more warily, such as Butch Cassidy and a companion, the Sundance Kid. There was an Opera House, a Naturatorium, and an Odd Fellows Lodge.

Today, tourists swim year-round in the private Tepee Pools, featuring a steam room and Jacuzzi; take in the newly remodeled Star Plunge with a 500-foot-long slide into hot mineral waters from the spring (50 cents a slide, 10 for $3.50); and enjoy the Holiday Inn, with weight and conditioning equipment, tanning booth and hot mineral Jacuzzi pool; all this in addition to the Hot Springs County Memorial Hospital also within the state park. An acre of green grass, a State Bath House, and the once beautiful travertine terraces along the Big Horn River, now dry and colorless—most of the algae-laden hot mineral waters are diverted to commercial users—are the remaining heritage of Chief Washakie. It is probably appropriate that the office of the Thermopolis Chamber of Commerce is also located within the state park.

LOCATED 177 MILES of highway northwest of Thermopolis is the world's first national park, Yellowstone, famed for its Old Faithful Geyser and a hundred lesser geysers, hot springs, and bubbling mud. No compromise with commercial use occurred in Yellowstone. From the very beginning of its establishment as a national park, it was determined that commercial activities would be subordinated to the spectacular natural beauty and geologic wonders.

The famous campfire story is well known, when members of the Washburn-Langford-Doane expedition on one of their final nights in the fantastic upland plateau they had been exploring decided that no part of the region should ever be privately owned, no homesteading or mining should occur, that the federal government should hold the land for-

Thermopolis Hot Springs source, Thermopolis, Wyoming. In discharge, this is reputed to be the largest hot springs in the world.

ever inviolate for use of the people. The principles guiding the creation of a national park system began around that campfire in Yellowstone.

No one believed the first descriptions of Yellowstone's geologic wonders (they were once called "Jim Bridger's lies"), but after photographs by Jackson quieted the doubters, an unexpected sense of responsibility arose in the halls of Congress at a time when free enterprise exploitation of the west was proceeding amok. In 1872, President Ulysses S. Grant signed the bill establishing the first national park, Yellowstone, "as a public park and pleasuring ground for the benefit and enjoyment of the people." Later, in 1890, the high Sierra lands around Yosemite Valley were brought into the embryonic national park system. Within twenty years, Sequoia, Mt. Rainier, Crater Lake, Wind Cave, and Mesa Verde were national parks, and California's

Yosemite State Park had belatedly joined the federal preserve system. Over the years, Yellowstone became the model for national parks around the world.

Indians in the region were crossing the area along the northern boundary en route to better bison hunting ranges to the west. Crow and Blackfeet controlled plains to the north and east and the Shoshone and Bannock tribes lived along the Snake River. Only a nomadic group of Shoshone, known as Sheepeaters, actually took up residence in the park area and endured the severe Yellowstone winters. They eked out a meager existence but were safe from more aggressive native American neighbors to the west.

Earthquakes in Yellowstone, as elsewhere, are often accompanied by roaring rumbles as faults twitch and rocks grind, and with the continuing background roar of geysers and slurp of boiling mud it is no wonder that early expeditions into the thermal region quoted Indians, saying, "they seldom go there because their children cannot sleep—and conceive it possessed of spirits, who were adverse that men should be near them." Yellowstone was not considered a desirable camping place by Indians, and when the federal government drew a boundary around the boiling and shaking plateau no Indian tribe made any prior claim.

It may have been the Sioux, whose word for "rock yellow water," or *Mitsladazi*, gave the name to Yellowstone. The French, *pierre jaune* or *roches jaunes*, meaning yellow rock or stone, was used by early trappers in the area to describe the exposed yellow stone in the canyon of the Yellowstone, and it is quite probable the name was passed on to visitors who arrived in increasing numbers to marvel at the geology where the wild west began beyond the plains.

Earthquakes are a commonly felt feature of pockmarked and fissured Yellowstone, averaging about five shakes a day. During an occasionally much agitated 24 hours, as much as 100 quivers may be measured by sensitive instruments, felt by no one. Most earthquakes are not strong enough to be mentioned on postcards mailed home, but near midnight on August 17, 1959, the fragile geologic structure of the region shifted along a fault ten miles beneath the surface. Suddenly the warm summer evening became a night of terror, killing 9 campers outright in a suffocating landslide. Some 19 others were never found.

An estimated 43.4 million cubic yards of rock slid from the ridge in one tremendous block into Madison Canyon several miles west of Yellowstone Park, burying the road, river, and campground under hundreds of feet of rubble a mile wide. The slide created a dam across the river, backing up the water and drowning the valley forest.

Within Yellowstone, rockslides buried many sections of park roads, collapsed a chimney over the dining hall at Old Faithful Lodge, and started 298 geysers and hot springs erupting, 160 having never erupted before. The earthquake measuring 7.1 on the Richter scale was exceeded in force by only fourteen previously recorded earthquakes in the United States. The energy released by the quake was equal to about 200 atom bombs of the type dropped on Hiroshima and was a frightening demonstration of the possibili-

ties for destruction in the peacefully steaming high plateau of Yellowstone.

At other times, the internal plumbing of Yellowstone, acting in its usually unpredictable fashion, will start or stop a geyser without warning. One of the most powerful geysers in Yellowstone, spouting not a drop of water since 1890, suddenly came back to life in 1985. Excelsior Geyser spewed steam and water to a height of 55 feet in the Midway Geyser Basin, then just as suddenly, two days later, quit.

Shoshone Indians celebrate the gift of the waters, Thermopolis Hot Springs.

Mammoth Hot Springs terrace, Yellowstone National Park, Wyoming.

Driving into Yellowstone country from the east, over paved roads from Buffalo Bill Cody's town, now called Cody, provides an opportunity to see the bizarre shapes of weathered and eroded mixed volcanic rocks and ash, the Absaroka topography. It's clear this is volcanic country, and a few miles farther west, past the park entry gate, the visual evidence is complete where a steaming vent on the shore of Yellowstone Lake provides an introduction to the high rolling plateau and a place to stand back and observe that much of Yellowstone is an ancient collapsed volcanic caldera, where magma is not far below the hot places above.

The land of bubbling mud, steaming pools, and spouting geysers covers one of the great volcanic areas of the world. No eruption has occurred in historical time, but molten rocks remain so close to the earth's surface that the possibility this weak place in the earth's crust may erupt again in the future cannot be disregarded. By any definition the geology of Yellowstone is a living geology where the eruption of scalding water may be but a precursor of more violent activity in the future, for Yellowstone straddles a series of overthrust faults extending through the Rocky Mountains in Montana to the Wasatch Range in Utah, where a great fault cliff is the backdrop to Salt Lake City. The collection of geysers, hot springs, mud pots, and fumaroles where the fault complex meets a major weakness in the earth's crust, the "hot spot" beneath the drifting continental plate in northwestern Wyoming, is the remnant of an ancient volcano that erupted about 600,000 years ago, burying thousands of square miles in hot ash as far away as Nebraska. The shifting faults still shake the earth, and Yellowstone ash is found throughout much of the western United States.

This eruption may have produced some of the earth's biggest explosions, with no counterpart in recorded history, even greater than the well-known destruction of Krakatoa Island between Java and Sumatra, an explosion heard 3,000 miles away in Australia. The Krakatoa eruption, for all its explosive force, produced a crater only a small fraction of the size of the collapsed caldera of Yellowstone, which is over 1,000 square miles in extent and several thousand feet deep. In one brief moment of geologic time there was launched in Yellowstone a chain of geologic events extending to today. Heat from the enormous reservoir of molten rock that produced the massive eruption still remains not too far below the earth's surface, sustaining Yellowstone's present thermal activity.

All the geyser activity occurs within the glacially eroded rim of the great caldera, where numerous underground fractures that carried lava to the surface after the eruption now provide subsurface channels for circulation of hot water in Yellowstone's thermal system. The only clearly identifiable remnant of the original caldera is the much smaller and younger inner caldera now flooded by the West Thumb of Yellowstone Lake and wreathed in steam plumes from vents along the shore.

The last lava flows from the caldera oozed from fractures about 70,000 years ago, preparing the surface for the estimated 2,500 individual thermal features in the national park, most clustered in a few geyser basins with continuous displays of intense thermal activity. Despite all the variable factors involved in geyser eruptions and changes that take place from time to time to alter the eruption patterns—such as earthquakes rearranging the subsurface glacial gravel carrying circulating water—Yellowstone geysers function regularly, day after day, week after week, year after year. Famous Old Faithful Geyser has not missed a single eruption in the many decades since it has been under close observation, although local earthquakes at times have jogged its internal plumbing system sufficiently to temporarily affect duration and height.

The floor of the ancient caldera began bulging upward about 150,000 years ago and two volcanic domes are now rising separately at a faster rate than the general Yellowstone uplift, the caldera area rising at the geologically rapid rate of about a half-inch per year. Along with this measured upward movement of central Yellowstone, reports during the past century noted more frequent earthquakes in the Yellowstone region than elsewhere in the Rocky Mountains. The earthquakes are fairly shallow, averaging around nine miles in depth at the upper limits of magma below, in some places less than four. Swarms of minor earthquakes also occur from time to time, indicating movement of magma beneath the ground where for several million years a body of molten magma has remained in place, capable of again erupting to the surface in a catastrophic explosion as it did so many thousands of years ago.

At present, the continental crustal plate is moving southwesterly over the Yellowstone "hot spot" in the earth's mantle, at the rate of about a half-inch per year, shifting the center of volcanic activity northeastward as the crust drifts to the southwest. Should this movement of the drifting continent continue, and it does seem probable as plate tectonics is generally understood, a new caldera may form in the northeastern corner of Yellowstone within the next several hundred thousand years. Yellowstone is still an area of potentially active volcanism. The next eruption may be in preparation.

CHAPTER EIGHT

Chasing the Hawaiian Goddess of Fire

Kapoho Volcano in eruption, Hawaii.

The revelatory, prescience *Kumu-lipo*—the thousand-year-old Hawaiian chant of creation—relates how the land grew up by itself; it was not created nor was it made by hand. As an excerpt from the *Kumulipo* reveals:

> *At the time when the earth became hot*
> *At the time when the heavens turned about*
> *At the time when the sun was darkened*
> *To cause the moon to shine*
> *The time of the rise of the Pleiades*
> *The slime, this was the source of the earth.*

In scholarly works charting pathways through obscure Hawaiiana, Martha Beck-with, translator of the *Kumulipo*, tells how traditional oral history, those so-called legends often rejected as fantastic myths, corresponds quite accurately with the Hawaiian view of the close relationship between nature and human beings—and in its own way expresses an apparent understanding of the earth's evolutionary formation before scientists provided confirming details.

The Hawaiian Islands, isolated as they are, provide a marvelous example of plate tectonics. The shifting crust of the earth reveals its evolutionary travel routes over the earth's molten interior, changing continuously the location of magnetic poles and continents, the edge of the seas, shape of the shore, and what appears to be a nomadic course of drifting Pacific islands.

Early Polynesians were aware of many geologic changes occurring over the years as they, too, migrated across Pacific water, populating the various groups of islands, most of them volcanic. Without scientific evidence to confirm assumptions, they called upon their demigod Maui, the Polynesian equivalent of the Greek Hercules, for explanation. Maui safely escorted pioneering Pacific travelers in outrigger canoes back and forth across the trackless oceans, and it was through Maui that island people understood the earth's behavior, whether it was the path of a distant star, the location of islands, or the length of a day.

Hawaiians offer a detailed explanation for the islands being located where they are, scattered about in the middle of the Pacific Ocean. In an ambitious undertaking that brought Maui into conflict with his contemporary One Tooth, a somewhat jealous supernatural being who was already assigned the task of keeping Pacific islands from drifting too close together or too far apart, Maui resolved to combine the Hawaiian Islands into unbroken land. Maui's mother suggested he look far offshore for help before meeting with One Tooth.

Sailing out on the ocean to where the islands were hazy on the horizon, Maui found a bailing calabash floating on the waves, and recognized it immediately as the help his mother had directed him to find. Scooping up the calabash, he paddled shoreward with his brothers, who had accompanied him to help pull in the catch. As they approached the islands, the calabash was transformed into a beautiful young mermaid, Hina, the Moon Lady. Before Maui could move toward her, the brown maiden vanished, leaving only the calabash in her place. Furious, Maui hurled the calabash overboard.

Maui's plan was to fish for One Tooth, hook him, and force him to release the islands. He took out his magic jawbone and tossed his fishing line into the ocean. The Moon Lady, out of the calabash again, was waiting below and pulled the hook under without revealing herself above the waves. She carried it deep into the sea until coming to One Tooth, whom she approached seductively. One Tooth was forced to smile and revealed his famous single tooth. Hina quickly tossed the hook down his throat, then threw two loops of coconut husk sennit around the lone tooth.

Kilauea Iki eruption, Hawaii Volcanoes National Park, Hawaii.

Maui, floating anxiously in the canoe above, felt the strike, secured the line, and exhorted his brothers to paddle with all their strength, warning them not to look back under any circumstances. The brothers paddled steadily to the northwest, in the same direction scientists would later learn was the path of the earth's shifting crust. They grew restless as Maui urged them on and soon could no longer restrain their curiosity. They glanced back and saw a string of islands—Hawaii, Maui, Molokai, Oahu, and Kauai—caught on Maui's line and splashing along behind his canoe.

The brothers shouted, "Look at what you've caught!" The spell was broken and the carefully placed hook slipped from One Tooth's mouth. The islands stopped in their forward movement, scattered, and slipped. They churned in the water, and Kauai and Niihau spun about together near the canoe. The line snapped and hurled the others farther away toward Tahiti, but One Tooth recovered his senses in time and caught Oahu as it began to float way, stopped Molokai from jamming into the island now bearing Maui's name, and was able to hold the Big Island of Hawaii in place over a hot place on the ocean seabed. Not daring to take further chances, One Tooth tied them all to the ocean floor in the places where they are today, with Hawaii Island still growing and fuming above the hot place on the ocean floor—the volcanic plume piercing the earth's mantle.

THE OLDEST HAWAIIAN ISLAND is the northernmost island, Kauai, which by no coincidence as far as native Hawaiians are concerned is also the original home of Pele, the Hawaiian Goddess of Fire and Volcanoes, a goddess feared and respected in ancient times and, for many, still feared today.

Pele manifested herself in many ways to the native Hawaiians, sometimes as a deity, dressing her hair to make it stand straight out from her head, inflaming and reddening her eyes, threatening commoners for favors—if not satisfied, they would be devoured. People had quite often seen with their own eyes Pele consume land, houses, and forests, even melt rocks, and the terror inspired by her was quite real. In later years, Hawaiians pleaded with Goddess Pele to shake loose molten lava from Mauna Loa's summit and wash hated foreign customs into the sea.

During the years after 1750, when High Chief Kamehameha was successfully conquering the islands one by one, Big Island Chief Keoua was returning to Ka'u after indecisive battles on the Hamakua coast when an explosive eruption at Kilauea filled the air with ash and poisonous gas not unlike the 1980 eruption of Mt. St. Helens. Just beyond Kilauea Crater some 400 of the fleeing army and their women and children were caught and suffocated as they fled the ash fallout. The tragedy was taken as an omen that Pele was on the side of Kamehameha; and the conqueror went on to win every island battle, uniting the islands into a single kingdom. The footprints of defeated Keoua's army, preserved in the hardened ash, can still be seen in the Ka'u desert. Kamehameha became king.

Following the missionaries' arrival in Hawaii, Kamehameha's favorite wife, Queen Kaahumanu, took the lead in overthrowing the ancient idols. But it was Queen Kapiolani who conceived the idea of helping establish Christianity by personally defying the Fire Goddess Pele on the very edge of Kilauea Volcano's firepit, Halemaumau.

As Queen Kapiolani camped for the night on the rim of Kilauea, several natives still obeisant to the old idols tried to dissuade her and predicted her death. She assured them otherwise, saying, "I should not die by your god. That fire was kindled by my God." In the morning, walking to the rim, a priestess again attempted to turn Kapiolani away, waving a piece of bark tapa, supposedly a palapala scroll from Pele. "I, too, have a palapala," responded Kapiolani, reading from a Hawaiian book of hymns and a classroom missionary spelling book.

Approaching the edge of the firepit, she broke off a branch of Pele's sacred o'helo berries, but, instead of sharing the ripe, red berries as traditional ritual prescribed by throwing half into the crater, she ate all the berries herself, refusing to share any with Pele. Then, calling out above the din of erupting lava in Kilauea's molten lake, she uttered her personal challenge, "Jehovah is my God. I fear not Pele." The frightened participants on the crater's rim were not overwhelmed by fire as expected, and the missionaries, relieved, returned to Hilo and full churches.

During the 1880 eruption of Mauna Loa,

when lava flowed rapidly toward Hilo Bay from a vent on the north flank, endangering residential communities above Hilo town—even the city itself—Princess Ruth, a granddaughter of King Kamehameha, then 63, was summoned to save the city. She proposed using the old, proven prayers to Pele, by then a heathen practice actively discouraged by the missionaries. The princess acquired a bottle of brandy, the only substitute she could find for the scarce *awa* made from hibiscus roots, and all the red handkerchiefs she could find. With her entourage following, she was carried overland up to the oncoming lava flow, her 400-pound queenly weight making it impossible for her to walk over the rough terrain.

Approaching the advancing lava front, Princess Ruth offered sacred chants to Pele, tossed the red kerchiefs one by one onto the lava flow, finally pouring brandy onto the dry *pulu* grass burning ahead of the flow. The next morning, Mauna Loa's erupting fountain was silent and the slowly moving lava had stopped at a stone wall on the edge of town.

Fifty years later, Hawaii was a territory of the United States, and when Hilo was again threatened by Mauna Loa's rampaging lava, Keystone bombers of the Army Air Corps were flown over from Honolulu to bomb erupting vents and disperse lava flows into cooling pools, despite dire predictions that Pele's wrath would descend upon the military pilots. Many local Hawaiians still claimed that Pele preferred alcoholic beverages and red handkerchiefs. In 1940, another eruption brought out Martin bombers from Honolulu. It is rumored that on this flight at least one Air Corps pilot dropped a bottle of Cutty Sark scotch with his bombs to ensure the mission's success, having been informed of Pele's preference.

I've talked with many residents of the Big Island who tell vivid stories of encountering Goddess Pele on narrow rural roads. Some of the first-person experiences are quite difficult to refute, although sightings of Pele commonly occur in the glow of eruptions and in the fading light of dusk when shadows can easily play tricks.

Pele, the goddess of fire, is still very much a part of Hawaiian lore, spoken of in reverence by the Hawaiians and invoked in many aspects of daily life, particularly on the Big Island where, during 1984–86, Kilauea

Kilauea Iki devastation trail, Hawaii Volcanoes National Park, Hawaii.

erupted repeatedly on virtually a monthly schedule, reminding everyone of Pele's ability to devour the landscape at will. Local residents, wanting Kilauea to perform for visiting outside-island friends, will often encourage Pele to erupt by offering a bottle of gin, thrown into the firepit with appropriate incantation. I did this once, and the next day was able to photograph a molten lava lake in Kilauea.

Pele's home, Kilauea Volcano and the southeastern rift flank, may be the most

Kilauea Iki eruption glowing in rain mist, Hawaii Volcanoes National Park, Hawaii.

active volcano in the world. It is also, perforce, the most gentle, allowing viewers to watch from the very edge of the crater even during its most active phases, when the erupting lava fountain may be higher than Chicago's Sears Tower.

In 1924, a violent steam explosion blew out the present Halemaumau firepit and drained what had been considered a permanent molten lava lake, a lake of fire attracting visitors from around the world to view the astounding sight from the Volcano House Hotel perched on the caldera rim. It was during this 1924 eruption that the only volcanic tourist fatality occurred in Hawaii. A falling rock ejected from Halemaumau hit a photographer and killed him.

IT WAS IN THE EARLY 1950s when I flew to Hawaii Island, having seen newspaper sto-

ries seeming to verify my amateur prognostications of a new outbreak in the eastern rift zone of Kilauea Volcano. Driving up the highway to talk with scientists at the Volcano Observatory, I encountered Dr. Gordon A. MacDonald a few miles from Hilo, and we waved each other to stop for a chat in the middle of the highway—Big Island style— where he advised that Puna was the place to watch.

I turned my rental car around and followed his station wagon to Pahoa town south across the rough, black lava fields of Puna, which produce sugarcane, wild orchids, and Ohi'a Lehua trees. A short distance beyond, we left our cars and walked into the nearby canefield where the earth was shaking noticeably and cracked and heaved before our eyes. Silently, as we watched in amazement, the earth split open, creating black pits large enough for a carport. Cracks continued opening into adjacent fields of young sugarcane, breaking apart the soil in long irregular lines scratched across the brown earth. Occasionally I could feel intermittent tremors through the soles of my boots as if somebody was trying to get out from beneath me. I stepped aside.

Civil defense police arrived and ordered me to leave, saying I was in an unsafe area and everyone, including residents and press, was being evacuated. I futilely explained this was why I was staying, but as more cracks opened between us he decided not to come closer and enforce his order. I stayed. I could see numerous picture oppotunities gradually developing around me as narrow cracks opened wider and new cracks exuded strange sulphurous smells. The earth below was creeping out.

I was prepared. My rented car was nearby, filled with a good quantity of film. Hanging cameras around my neck, I carefully stepped over cracks before they opened too wide, photographing narrow hairline breaks spreading in the dry dirt into the rift area. I felt strangely unafraid, waiting for some-

thing I knew would happen. The police and other people I had seen shortly before had disappeared. I could no longer see Dr. MacDonald and was pleased I had left my car back at the road junction when a nearby crack slowly spread wide enough to swallow a light truck. I stepped back. I might miss photographing the end of the world, but I was certainly going to stay around for what appeared to be a new beginning.

The clear air suddenly became cloudy as I stared and watched straight ahead of me— wisps of steam vapor puffing from a new crack clotting swiftly into a column of thick smoke. I retreated momentarily, watching small globs of orange, molten rock begin spurting into the air, pushing apart the lengthening crack as the black interior of the earth melted into bright red and overflowed at my feet. I took more pictures and stepped farther back when increasing heat from lava geysers rapidly began building a small spatter cone around the now-roaring volcanic vent. Molten lava at the vent exceeded temperatures of over 2,000° Fahrenheit.

Ohia lehua trees killed by Kilauea Iki in eruption with Mauna Loa in the distance, Hawaii Volcanoes National Park.

Kilauea Iki, Hawaii Volcanoes National Park, Hawaii.

I felt there was little danger from the lava as long as I could see the opening vents, but as advancing clouds of fume blanketed the area I became concerned over what I could not see, even wondering what might happen to my car, since I could no longer find it in the haze. Could it have fallen into one of the larger cracks? I was wondering what Avis would say when I reported their car had disappeared into the earth when a sudden shift of the light wind blew dense clouds of sul-

phurous smoke directly toward me. I saw the cloud coming but could not avoid it. With the next lungful of air my throat suddenly contracted shut as I sucked in hot sulfur fumes. I couldn't breathe! The sudden realization that volcanoes were deadly frightened me into running as fast as possible away from the vents to escape poisonous gases rapidly enveloping the area. I ran to windward like a track star until I collapsed in the clear, breathing deep gulps of fresh air as I lay on the ground. It was a lesson to be appreciated and remembered. When I again photographed volcanoes, I carefully stayed upwind.

As the erupting vent grew into lava fountains a hundred feet high amid every indication they would be considerably higher within hours, lava began flowing downslope toward the sea, covering adjacent canefields, the heat wilting young cane stalks and setting them afire before burying them, blistering paint off the walls of nearby plantation housing before they, too, burst into flame and burned to the ground. Residents ran from their homes with what they hoped were their most valuable possessions, waiting until the last moment to flee. I watched with morbid curiosity then retreated, escaping by driving down a plantation road with mature tasseled cane blazing on each side like a wild forest fire. I parked my smoky car in a clearing below the erupting fissure. So I might photograph the oncoming lava flow head on, I scouted the terrain carefully to determine where the lava would flow next, reconnoitering new escape routes should another hasty retreat become necessary.

Late in the afternoon, I became aware I was alone with the volcano. The few plantation houses were gone, I had not seen scientist MacDonald for hours, and not even normally inquisitive newspeople or photographers arrived to photograph what I began to call my volcano, an eruption that by now was putting on a rather spectacular show in the dramatic late afternoon light. Apparently plantation roads were blocked by police who were barring entry of reporters and photographers to an area considered dangerous, and they were unaware that I was inside the forbidden zone. Wonderful! I had the volcano all to myself—a photographic scoop. I savored the thought with great relish. All I needed to do was keep my location secret, continue photographing, and keep my car away from the still-advancing lava flow. Fortunately, I knew the country back roads well, probably better than city police manning roadblocks. Moving my car to a hard-to-see location under a nearby grove of mango trees, I waited for sunset, the best time of day other than dawn to photograph volcanoes displaying their awesome beauty. It had become my task to challenge the volcano and the police, those who would keep me away from my personal encounter with the shaking earth.

Well after dark, I left the car and walked directly *makai*—toward the sea—bearing slightly westward toward a small cluster of lights perhaps a mile away. Crossing the plowed canefields, I stumbled several times in the darkness but was reasonably success-ful in finding my way in the volcano's off-and-on glow, not wanting to use a flashlight to advertise my presence. I passed a small group of shadowy people without turning any heads, then circled around to approach them from the rear, walking like a homeless ref-ugee up to a Red Cross station wagon dis-pensing donuts and coffee. Innocently I inquired how I could get nearer the eruption. A friendly policeman replied I was already as close as I was going to get. "No one," he said, "not even the press, is allowed any closer by order of civil defense."

I filled myself with Red Cross coffee, stuffed my pockets with extra donuts to enjoy by myself under the mango trees, and qui-etly joined in conversation with several freelance photographers and reporters grum-bling about undue restrictions imposed upon the working press. Without complaining too much, I disappeared into the darkness, found my car, and curled up on the back seat in the volcano's reflected glow, hoping I had suffi-cient film and thinking of ways and means of getting my exclusive photo coverage back to *Life* magazine in time for Thursday's deadline. My car was on a high spot in the canefield, and I fell asleep confident that any lava flows changing direction during the night would flow past and not over me.

One story I heard while accepting my share of Red Cross donuts continued to intrigue me as I listened to the characteristic crack and tinkle of lava slowly pushing through the canefield, an almost musical counter-point to the steady, subdued roar from the erupting volcanic vent. Ola'a Sugar Com-pany, whose canefields were being burned and buried, received a negative reply from its New

York insurance company upon requesting payment for sugarcane destroyed by cane fire. The insurance company claimed the sugar was buried by lava and not burned, therefore Ola'a was not covered under its policy. At Ola'a Sugar's insistence, a claims agent was flown to the Hawaiian Islands and driven to the eruption so he could see firsthand how the cane caught fire and burned before it was buried. As the claims agent was driven closer and closer to the erupting vents, he became more and more agitated and frightened; finally, on the verge of apoplexy, as the lava

Halemaumau firepit and Kau Desert ash and cinder, Kilauea Crater, Hawaii Volcanoes National Park, Hawaii.

Highway junction, Puna, Hawaii.

fountain roared straight ahead, he agreed to all that Ola'a contended—just as long as they took him away from those mad volcano watchers.

The roar that never varies, never hesitates, is the most disturbing sound to sleep by, confirming the continuing cosmic power of the lava being released in violent ferment. The volcano's throat is a rocket's jet, thrusting yellow-orange, molten rock out of the vent at blurred speed. The lava falls back to earth in arcs of cooling shapes and cinder chunks, changing quickly in color like sparkling confetti from orange to red to cold black when the rock melts back into the night. I knew in the morning I would be able to find thin ribbons made in the lava fountains and blown by the wind into shapes so fragile they soon wither away. To the Hawaiians, the golden threads are Pele's hair, the glassy droplets, Pele's tears. In the throbbing darkness beyond the volcano's glow, a breeze surrounded me with sulphurous air, reminding me of my first encounter with Pele and that an integral part of this mesmerizing beauty is asphyxiation and death.

The Puna lava fountain steadily grew in size, reflecting a bright orange-red glow into my car—enough to read by. I turned my head to watch the grand volcanic display not a half mile away, a pulsating apparition in the night, its blinding glare smothering the stars, casting trees into ghostly silhouettes hovering at the fringes of the volcano's brightness.

As I dozed off, I was not unaware that I should also be concerned about a possible errant lava flow moving in my direction, that widening cracks could open farther along Kilauea's Puna rift, even beneath my car, bringing to life new lava with which to contend.

I awoke with a start, reacting spontaneously to an explosion downhill from the car, and immediately started the engine. I

Kilauea Iki, Hawaii Volcanoes National Park, Hawaii.

looked around. Lava flowed by on both sides of my little hill. The only uncovered earth was straight ahead, an escape route rapidly being cut off as the lava flows edged together. Another explosion diverted my attention—my wake-up call was 55-gallon steel drums of chemical herbicide exploding and splitting open loudly as molten lava surrounded the barrels, heating them to the ignition point. I eluded the lava flow's molten tongue on the last road in the area still uncovered, driving again down a narrow cinder road among burning sugarcane and exiting without incident from the blazing tunnel of fire trailing soot and burning trash, although my rental car was missing a radio antenna and some unnecessary grillwork and had accumulated a considerable number of deep scratches in the blistered paint.

In the afternoon, I met the *Life* photographer sent out from New York, who had not been allowed to enter within photographing distance of the eruption, turned over my film for him to send on, and returned to the volcano, finding my way back on the roads I knew so well. No one tried to follow me, apparently having noted the disreputable appearance of my car and deciding it was not where they wanted to go. Maybe Avis told them not to.

The earth split open again that night, in the east, across the empty Pahoa-Kapoho paved road. A long crack opened in the dark, spurting a curtain of fire a half-mile in length in a sudden swish across the hillside like a broken black-powder firecracker. The lava fountains lasted for not more than an hour, retreating back into the earth to leave behind a black scar exposed in the morning sun, a cold, hardened, lava-spattered crack in the red earth.

The new lava landscape was cold when several years after the Puna rift split open the plantation village of Kapoho was awakened by harmonic tremors warning of a new eruption farther along Kilauea's active rift. The bright green expanses of freshly mowed lawn fronting whitewashed sugar company housing in Kapoho were broken apart by the earthquake's black scars, exposing the earth beneath as residents hurried in and out, loading pickups with personal household goods—mattresses, beds, cribs, chairs, and sofas piled high on the smallest trucks. Children clutched their toys and climbed into the small fleet of cars and trucks carrying away mov-

Constructing rock dikes in an unsuccessful attempt to prevent the village of Kapoho from being buried by lava flow.

able property belonging to the sugar workers and farmers of Kapoho. They were perhaps unaware of the fact, but this would be the last time they would see their homes for within a few weeks all Kapoho would burn to the ground as lava flows buried the town, the familiar playgrounds, backyards, and streets, restoring the landscape to its original appearance before people deigned to live atop volcanoes.

Kapoho eruption, Hawaii.

Kapoho afire.

The Kapoho eruption began above town in a papaya orchard—lava fountains in the rift crack swiftly moving seaward, then coming to a halt in the canefield beyond Y. Nakamura's general store and gas station. Nakamura was growing vanda orchids for tourists and had just completed nailing down the galvanized steel roof on a new home for his children. The walls of the house were not yet set up—they were to be installed last in the manner of traditional island single-wall structures—and he could easily look through the house from his store and see the new mountain rising in his backyard.

Day by day, the new volcano grew, sending great quantities of cinders into the sky, mostly carried by wind in an easterly direction, but occasionally to the west where late one night falling hot cinders effectively removed most of the paint from my rental car and encouraged me to purchase a protective hard hat. Increasing quantities of lava poured from the vent; a river of molten rock

flowed into the ocean only two miles away, where billowing clouds of steam rushing into the sky created local weather unusual for Hawaii: one afternoon hail fell from the skies above Kapoho. Fishermen caught boiled fish. In the second week, groundwater entered the erupting vent, resulting in a continuous explosion of steam and rock into the sky; the roar was heard for miles.

The governor declared an emergency when the lava river overflowed and threatened to cover the town. Volcanologists and civil defense people conferred, decided an earthen dike might possibly deflect lava away from Kapoho, and called for every bulldozer on the island to assemble at the eruption for a most unusual construction job—the erection of a levee 1 mile long averaging 15 feet and more in height, made of earth and rock scraped from the site.

I was hired by the state to quickly photograph every building in Kapoho. If the state was going to be sued because of an experi-

Nakamura store, Kapoho. The Kilauea east rift eruption reaches groundwater.

mental levee raised overnight, they wanted some evidence of what the buildings might have been worth.

Bulldozers of every size and color arrived by trailer and went to work immediately, first smashing flat the Ohi'a Lehua Forest. Then under the frantic direction of sugar plantation *lunas* who were not quite sure what they were doing, pushed dirt, splintered logs, and rocks into the planned barrier between Kapoho town and the approaching lava flow. All night they worked, and into the next day, the eruption's roar mixed with the clanking squeaking of Caterpillar threads and the rattle of snorting diesel engines. The volcano's sulphurous fumes diluted with smoky diesel exhaust permeated a tortured landscape looking not unlike a battlefield.

The village of Kapoho on fire and buried by lava flow.

On the second day, they rested and waited, in some ways confident of success, while lava climbed higher and higher against their impromptu barrier, some 15 feet wide and twice as high in places. It seemed impenetrable, but when victory appeared most evident, when cold beer was being shared by tired and dusty bulldozer operators, Goddess Pele surprised everyone by pushing her lava underneath the dike! Tremendous pressure exerted by the fluid mass of molten rock, like water behind a dam, simply punched out wet soil beneath the levee as if nothing were there. The lava did not divert; it went under and formed a new flow beyond the now useless dike. Pele was not to suffer any detours on her inexorable journey to the sea.

First to burn was Kapoho School as the lava began encroaching upon the town. Next, the post office. Individual houses caught fire as the searing heat from approaching lava set dry wood aflame in sudden flashes of smoke and sparks. City firemen from Hilo, under orders to put out the fires, laid new hoses from nearby hydrants as fast as irate homeowners chopped holes in them with machetes, wanting their homes to burn before being buried under lava. They had paid for fire insurance; there was no lava insurance. One by one, almost all the buildings of Kapoho burned and in turn were buried. In one night, Kapoho was gone. There were no more pictures to be made, so I drove to Hilo and returned my rental car. Avis refused to take it back, saying they hadn't rented me a wreck. *Life* magazine never printed my pictures of Kapoho—no one had died.

Lava continued flowing into the sea, a black, steaming point of new land extending foot by foot out into the ocean. When the Kapoho eruption on Kilauea's flank finally ended, Hawaii was 600 feet closer to California.

THE ERUPTION AT KAPOHO broke out on the lower eastern rift of Kilauea Volcano, a rift extending from the central Kilauea caldera in Hawaii Volcanoes National Park into the sea beyond Kapoho at Kumukahi. Kilauea most recently erupted from a vent high on the rift, sending lava flows into the ocean across uninhabitated national park lands below Holei Pali and onto populated areas west of the small community of Kalapana at Kaimu.

Nearing Kalapana in the winter of 1986, a seven-mile river of molten lava from the Kilauea rift overran speculative subdivisions bulldozed out of several-hundred-year-old lava flows, all within sight of the erupting vent of Puu O'o. Volcanologists had been privately concerned when longtime island residents and then mainlanders not altogether acquainted with the erratic behavior of Hawaii volcanoes, began buying lots in the threatened Kalapana area to "own a piece of paradise," as aggressive salesmen called the opportunity. Buying vacant lava land, they began to build their homes in an area clearly in the path of future lava flows. Environmentalists who wanted the sparsely forested lands kept in open space for possible expansion of the national park were appalled when subdivisions were approved and residential building permits issued. The county government seemed unconcerned. It was another example of people refusing to recognize the dangers of living on an active volcano or on active earthquake fault areas. It was their own decision—a chance they would readily take to live in one of the most pleasant regions of the Big Island. They lost. In the last month of 1986 most of the new homes were set afire and buried by 2,000° Fahrenheit lava.

"We'll have to let Pele do what she wants to do," said Hawaii County Mayor Dante Carpenter, referring to the Hawaiian goddess of the volcano.

Some oldtime residents were also caught in the spreading lava flow and lost their homes. Families that have lived in Kalapana for generations, families that have roots, were born and raised unafraid in the glow of Kilauea volcano.

"Pele adds to the land, until it gets bigger and bigger," commented lifelong resident Sam Kaaualoa, whose home was destroyed when lava flowed to the sea. "I guess Pele goes on and on until she figures enough is enough."

While Kilauea continued to pump magma high on the volcano's flank, lava broke out of hardened tubes during the week to spread out and stagnate in the upland forest, sparing nearly 100 other homes and the small wood-framed Star of the Sea Catholic Church built on ancient lava flows along the shore at Kaimu.

"I didn't think we would have Mass this Sunday," Father Larry Burns told about 80

Pahoehoe lava with first growing fern, Hawaii.

members of his parish. "Thank God we are here again together and thank God our little church was spared."

Accompanied by ukulele and guitar, the worshipers sang Hawaiian hymns and held hands as they celebrated Mass while lava from Kilauea Volcano cooled outside, near where someone had placed an offering to appease the Goddess Pele, a fifth of gin wrapped in leaves of a ti plant along with a piece of carved koa wood.

After the current eruption phase has ended and the lava hardened, many residents of Kalapana will be rebuilding atop their old homesteads.

CHAPTER NINE

Volcanoes and the Devil

Mango tree with Kilauea lava fountain, Hawaii.

Mark Twain told of the continuing relationship between the devil and volcanoes when he described Hawaii's volcanic firepit Halemaumau: "The smell of sulphur is strong, but not unpleasant to a sinner."

From the time that early people first reacted to the spectacular sight of a volcano in eruption and talked about it, an astonishing variety of writers, poets, philosophers, and just plain people have been afflicted emotionally by the strong impression volcanic activity has on everyone. Many have passed on their reaction to the spiritual power apparently emanating from within volcanoes. Primitive tribes have passed down oral descriptions of strange encounters and a multitude of legends proving the influence of volcanic activity and high volcanic peaks on their lives. There appears to be a special quality about volcanoes, a "holy planet" to many, that exudes an abundance of spiritual activity and esoteric revelations self-proclaimed by prophets and oracles who have enumerated a plethora of visionary encounters and adventures to test the imagination of the most gullible. Volcanic peaks are indeed mountains to be reckoned with.

California and the west, split by faults and pock-marked by dormant volcanoes, are considered to be populated by "flakes" by many living east of the western edge, yet it was a Chicago paperhanger out hiking on the slopes of northern California's Mt. Shasta, a dormant volcano, who saw the light, met a reincarnated St. Germain, traveled the world with him, and on returning to Shasta City in the 1930s founded the I AM religion. It still thrives today and regularly broadcasts by radio what it believes to be the true words passed down by St. Germain on Mt. Shasta.

Just as some travelers have received cryptic messages on the mountain in the same manner that Moses received the Ten Commandments, others tell the mountains what to do, viewing life on earth as controlling geologic forces, moving tectonic plates, and changing atmospheric and oceanic chemistry, a sort of sentient life force governing the planet. The concept is ascribed to Gaia, the ancient Greek goddess of the earth.

While those involved in the occult might prefer Gaia to the devil, geologist Steven Austin, keynote speaker at a California Creationist Conference and self-described catastrophist, says that the study of natural events such as the eruption of Mt. St. Helens can ultimately disprove evolution and yield proof that the world was created all at once just as Genesis says it was.

"We don't know what controls these volcanoes; we don't know who or what controls nature," Austin said. "But events such as Mt. St. Helens are a testimony to the power of nature in our lives—and it gets people thinking about who really is in control." Austin said his research on Mt. St. Helens proves to him that coal can be formed in a relatively short time, only a few thousand years instead of billions as most scientists estimate. He stopped short of claiming that God triggered the Mt. St. Helens eruption but was familiar with Psalm 104, verse 32: "He looks upon the earth and it trembles; He touches the hills and they smoke."

There are not, to my knowledge, any earthquake cults, such as might be called the California Shakers or Defaulters, but in the state of Washington the eruption of Mt. St. Helens has encouraged the reporting of instant legends and stories of a giant human walking about in the winter snows. He's been named, appropriately, Bigfoot, and a small cafe at Cougar, nearest town to Mt. St. Helens, has an actual cast of Bigfoot's foot mounted on the wall behind the serving counter. The waitress will authenticate the imprint if you ask.

Within sight of the Columbia River, where its spectacular gorge breaks through the otherwise continuous range of Cascade peaks, are three volcanoes: Mt. Hood, Mt. Adams,

The underworld at the surface in Norris Geyser Basin, Yellowstone National Park, Wyoming.

Morro Rock at Morro Bay, an ancient volcano core, California.

and Mt. St. Helens, which were named Wy'east, Pahto, and La-wa-la-clough by local Indians living in the area before white settlers intruded. According to the storytellers, these mountains fought each other constantly, and on one occasion when the female mountain let it be known that she preferred Pahto to Wy'east, the peak now called Adams was hit so hard by Hood in the resulting scuffle that it forever remained somewhat flattened, never recovering the graceful symmetrical cone shape of its more handsome brothers and sisters.

Other mountains in the region, perhaps because they often erupted violently from time to time, are also associated with tales of fights and squabbling. Yakima Indians, living in the ashy fallout shadow of Mt. St. Helens, relate stories about the Great Chief Above and how the earth was made as we know it, creating a man made out of a ball of mud and, when the man became lonely,

making a woman to live with him. The Great Chief Above taught them how to do everything necessary to live on earth; but in spite of this, the people quarreled and bickered so much that Mother Earth became angry and shook the mountains so roughly that rocks falling into the water dammed the streams and made waterfalls, rapids, and lakes where none existed before, and many wild animals and people were killed and buried under the rocks and sliding earth.

Elder Yakima tribal members say that someday the Great Chief Above will again shake the mountains and overturn them, and that the spirits once living in the bones of those buried there, who in life kept the beliefs of their grandparents, will go back into the bones. These spirits presently live on the mountain summits, from where they observe their children below, awaiting the great change that will surely come. They say the voices of the spirits can be easily heard in the high mountain wilderness when a visitor to the high places stops to listen.

A RELATIVELY QUIET VOLCANIC PEAK in the southern Cascades has continued to be of significance to people who have listened to the mountain, apparently received a message, and imagined much more. Mt. Shasta in northern California, as the Shasta Indians relate in their stories about the volcano— the mountain made before any other mountain—is described by geologists as actually four separate volcanoes that erupted at different times, atop and against each other, combining together into one of the largest volcanoes of its kind in the world, a snow-capped mountain above the surrounding forest. Shasta dominates the northern California landscape like no other mountain and, more significantly than lesser Lassen Peak

to the south, dramatically identifies the geological transition between the Sierra and the Cascades. It is often first seen driving north in the Sacramento Valley when there remain yet a hundred miles left to travel.

Closer, the mountain's immense bulk is impressive, more to some viewers than others. More than any other mountain on the continental edge, it has inspired a bewildering assemblage of cults, sects, and religious devotees imputing some remarkable events to its spiritual presence.

All this started, as the Shasta Indian people relate it, when the Great Spirit Above looked below and, seeing the land was flat, made a hole in the sky and pushed ice and snow down to earth until the highest mountain was created. Additional snow and ice were piled on to raise the top above the clouds, and trees were made to grow around the lower slopes. It is said the Great Spirit Above called the mountain Shasta because the peak was white and pure.

Spirit Lake after Mt. St. Helens eruption, Mt. St. Helens National Monument, Washington.

Later arrivals in California decided Mt. Shasta had not come from the sky, and they quoted their own sources proclaiming Mt. Shasta as "the last refuge of the survivors of the lost continent of Lemuria." According to the published Rosicrucian version of this tale, "all the thousands of large and small islands in the Pacific Ocean are mountain peak remnants of the submerged continent" of Lemuria. The eastern shore of this ancient continent consisted, it is said, of the coastal lands west of the Sierra and Cascade mountains and is all that remains after the continent sank from sight, leaving behind "the oldest of living things, the oldest of cultivated soil, and . . . numerous relics of the human race which had reached a higher state of cultural development and civilization than any other races of man." The Rosicrucian mystics, who wrote that they personally examined historical records of the Lemurians, also described their travels thousands of years ago in "an airship which looked just a little like our modern blimp," often flying, as they wrote, between their continent and Atlantis on the other side of the earth. Lemuria was destroyed, according to the Rosicrucians, by cataclysmic upheavals and volcanic eruptions that also consumed most of the Lemurian race, except for a few able to escape and establish colonies in the area surrounding Mt. Shasta. They write of the event as the great flood, the same flood described in the Bible, that forced survivors to flee to the nearby summit of Mt. Shasta.

Aficionados of Atlantian and Lemurian tales often equate the lost continent of Lemuria with the oceanic continent of Mu, shown on maps prepared by archaeologist James Churchward to validate his hypothesis of Mu as the "mother" of several colonial civilizations that spread around the Pacific Rim. Churchward identified close connections with what eventually became known as Oregon, Shasta, and Teotihuacán in central Mexico.

Shasta City, Mt. Shasta, northern California.

Inscribed tablets found northwest of Mexico City in 1921 were said by Churchward to contain sacred, inspired writings from the lost continent of Mu, which had disappeared about 12,000 years ago, about the same time that Atlantis went down in the Atlantic. Churchward said the tablets originated in Tibet. Academics threw up their hands and refused to recognize the tablets as anything but forgeries when Churchward said they took the history of man back 200,000 years and described in detail life on the continent of Mu, which at one time extended 6,000 miles across the Pacific on both sides of the equator. Stone-lined canals and walled temple-fortresses, said by Churchward to be described on the tablets, can be seen today on Ponape Island in Micronesia, islands that Churchward never visited.

In past years, reports by travelers in the region of Shasta have mentioned seeing odd-looking persons who ran back into hiding when seen, people "distinctive in features and complexion ... having the appearance of being quite old and yet exceedingly agile." Inquisitive outsiders attempting to venture into the forest to investigate strange lights and sounds, according to Rosicrucian accounts, have been bodily lifted from the ground and turned away or sometimes forced to remain fixed in place by a "peculiar set of vibrations or invisible energy." Other representatives of these lost people of Lemuria or Mu have been seen in Shasta City "garbed in pure white and in sandals, with long curly hair, tall and majestic in appearance."

Another writer in a Rosicrucian magazine came to the conclusion, after listening in vain for strange sounds and searching for lights on Mt. Shasta, that there are no Lemurians on the mountain, or temples or ruins either, and he never found the storekeeper who reputedly exchanged merchandise for gold nuggets with strange inhabitants of the forest.

The writer John P. Scott did say, however, that he was told there are unusual mineral deposits and peculiar physical formations on the mountain that when combined with certain air currents produce strange effects, even ghostly sounds. He wrote that the phenomenon was mostly physical and difficult to see because the average person doesn't consider ethers as being physical since "one cannot see them and knows nothing of them." Scott said that ancient people still do live on Mt. Shasta, and he believes they could be con-

tacted under the right conditions by the right people. They are, he said, "earthbound spirits from an old civilization which once existed in this locality, and they're still up there." Scott agreed that Mt. Shasta seems to definitely be a sensitive spot, where it is "easier to contact those on other planes than most other places."

In addition to the Rosicrucians, there are the Ancient Mystical White Brotherhood After the Order of Mechizedek, the white apparently referring to Shasta's perpetual snow; the Colorado-based Knights of the White Rose; the Radiant School of the Seekers and Servers; the Brotherhood of Mt. Shasta; and the Ascended Masters and Cosmic Beings of I AM, the largest of Shasta's many sects. I AM has published detailed accounts of incredible happenings on Mt. Shasta in 1930, when a reincarnated St. Germain appeared from the sky to meet with his appointed earthly prophet, Guy Ballard, hiking on a Shasta trail overlooking the McCloud River Valley. St. Germain asked for the hiker's empty drinking cup and instantly it was filled with a delicious creamy liquid having an "electrical vivifying effect." He was described by Ballard as a "magnificent Godlike figure—in a white jeweled robe, light and love sparkling in his eyes...."

Using Mt. Shasta as a base, the hiker and the spirit traveled around the world by simply rising rapidly into space, eventually ending up in Wyoming's Grand Tetons where they entered the summit interior, walking through a large bronze door in the highest peak that, according to St. Germain, "has been here since before the sinking of Atlantis, more than 12,000 years ago." He went on to explain how Yellowstone was named, telling about extensive gold mines and yellow diamonds found in that hot place long ago. It is clearly evident that mountains and volcanoes can do audacious things to the imagination, probably because of the hallucinations produced by altitude sickness and overexposure to the sun or the light air and fumes wafting around volcanic peaks.

The Knights of the White Rose offer a different explanation for the strange lights seeming to emanate from Mt. Shasta. It seems the Lemurians were captured by people from the lost continent of Atlantis, who held them captive in a cave under some islands in Micronesia in the central Pacific. The flashing lights are said to be Atlantean spacecraft coming and going from their fortress deep within the mountain. Other explanations for the lights are as mundane as they are perplexing. Geophysicists have given papers citing evidence that small earthquakes and underground strain may be the cause of lights viewed for years by awed eyewitnesses. Reports of eerie lights—often resembling glowing baseballs floating among treetops—have decreased since Mt. St. Helens erupted, suggesting that relief of internal pressures has stopped flammable gas from escaping through ground cracks. Another possibility is that "the cracking ground releases high-energy electric particles from rocks, and that the particles somehow gather into visible balls of energy." The scientific reasoning presented at an American Geophysical Society meeting in itself calls for further elucidation. The assumption might be made that when otherwise unaccountable lights on Mt. Shasta glow brighter, it may be time to consider the likelihood of an eruption.

An estimated 40 to 50 cult groups attach spiritual significance to Mt. Shasta. They describe 15 to 20 kinds of strange beings living inside or somewhere on the mountain. Some believe a race of dwarfs similar to Hawaiian *menehunes* or Irish leprechauns inhabit Shasta.

According to Ray Miller, a retired Navy intelligence officer who lives nearby, "There's a group on the north side of Shastina that must be the world's greatest bellmakers. I've been told they've hollowed out Shastina (one of Shasta's two summits) and have this big invisible bell hanging outside the mountain that repels people they don't want to see."

Long before the California-based Rosicrucians had postulated accounts of a lost continent and the secret commonwealth people claimed to occupy underground homes actually inside Mt. Shasta in the legendary cities of Iletheleme and Yaktayvia—occupying an interior below the earth drained of lava—a new religion, Christianity, was getting organized in Palestine with a Bible telling of an underworld filled with molten lava, a lake of fire they called Hell.

The idea of punishment in Hell apparently began with the Egyptians, who cremated their dead at sunset—the "pit of fire" as they called it. Later, in the valley of Hinnom south of Jerusalem, human sacrifices were offered to the pagan god and dead bodies were thrown and burnt there. The ancients didn't view the underworld as a place of punishment. It was dark, mysterious, and awesome but not the vast torture chamber Christians later made of the place beneath.

HELL IS PERHAPS the most sadistic fantasy ever conceived. It is described, painted, and contemplated with incredibly perverse relish as a perpetual lake of volcanic fire down below, an eternal fire where inextinguishable flames burn forever. To a Christian and a geologist, it is a reasonable description of the earth below, and it is understandable how the ancient god of fire, Vulcan, in such uncontrolled manifestations as the volcanoes that perpetuate his name, has come to be associated with the ultimate punishment of sinners and unbelievers.

St. John the Divine wrote of these retributions in Chapter 20 of Revelations, where he warns of a "fiery lake of burning brimstone" and how "the fire came down from heaven and consumed them, and the devil who led them astray was flung into the fiery, sulphurous lake, where the animal and the false prophet were, there to be tortured day and night forever and ever." St. John could have only been thinking of a volcanic lake of fire below the earth, as he continued, "They were all judged by what they had done. Then death and Hades [Roman god of the lower world] were flung into the fiery lake. Anyone whose name was not found written in the book of life was flung into the fiery lake."

The volcanic connection undoubtedly originates with the early Greco-Roman gods of mythology. Hades was the hidden god in the "womb of the earth" and Vulcan was god of volcanic fire. Vulcan's own forge was thought to be below Mt. Aetna or Mt. Vesuvius. His assistants, too, had their smithies underground, and the heat and sparks belched forth as volcanoes.

The devil is said to be the partner of death and sinners. To dream of the devil means trouble, it is also said. If he appears in fire, some immediate misfortune can be expected; if he vanishes in smoke, returning calm will occur. It is the devil that escorts the sinner to hell, and paintings of Hell and lakes of fire almost always show the devil in attendance. The devil's bed is brimstone.

Mango tree in volcano glow, Kapoho, Hawaii.

The devil and sulfurous lakes of fire are like Hades and Hell, Christian liturgical symbols that have become American folklore. As frontiersmen traveled west, away from a friendly eastern seaboard of gentle hills and meandering streams, they encountered the wild west, a land not only of Indians but of grotesque landscapes and rock formations that could only be ascribed to the devil's handiwork. So many of these landmarks were of both ancient and recent volcanism that the link with a fiery underworld became obvious, and geographic identification on maps was construed as a catalog of the devil's work. But even the most sophisticated explorer will often describe awesome vistas in terms of the nether world, as Jacques Cousteau did on his television segment describing the summit crater on Deception Island in Antarctica: "It is satanic, like Hell frozen over."

The devil as an undesirable opponent to the white man was apparently understood by the Black Hills Indians who, when asked about their land by early Americans entering the territory in violation of Indian treaty rights, affected a calculated silence, hoping the whites would leave, telling them only that the huge volcanic obelisk rising from the surrounding plains was the Devil's Tower. If the name was meant to scare off the white explorers and those to follow, it did not.

To the Indians this dramatic volcanic upthrust of rock marked the dwelling place of bears. They called the tower *Mateo Tepee,* or Bear Lodge, telling stories of lost children who were chased by a giant bear and climbed on top of a rock in a last desperate effort to save themselves. The children appealed to the spirits and the rock rose up out of the ground, lifting the youngsters beyond the bear's reach. It was the bear's futile attempt to claw its way to the top that left permanent grooves around the tower—the columnar basaltic rocks seen today.

Approaching the rock tower, destined to become the nation's first national monument, from far away it is noticed that something isn't right. The tower rises perpendicularly from the flat landscape like a mistake, a geological orphan that doesn't belong anywhere around northeastern Wyoming. Among the mountains of the west the scalped peak would be out of place, and it was some time before geologists identified the stone mesa

Columnar basalt, Devil's Postpile National Monument, California.

for what it was, the cold core of a volcano that filled to the brim of an ancient vent but never erupted. The earth around eroded away, leaving Devil's Tower alone on the midcontinent prairie.

IN CALIFORNIA, the stacked basaltic logs near the volcanic Mammoth Lakes area are called the Devil's Postpile. All over the west are other manifestations of the underworld: the Devil's Cauldron in Yellowstone, Devil's Barbecue Pit in Idaho, Devil's Punchbowl in Oregon, and in California the Devil's Den, Playground, Golf Course, Homestead, Cornfield, Kitchen, Racetrack, Slide, and even the Devil's Heart in Los Padres National Forest.

While Christians were describing an underworld occupied by the devil and eternal lakes of fire, a Hell on earth, native American Indians expressed the universal concern with fundamental issues in a fantastic spectrum of forms, heroes, and tricksters living in worlds piled on top and inside each other, of perpetual danger and re-creation in terms of the natural world around them. Their imagination knew no limits. Their stories were magic lenses through which they could glimpse social orders and daily life related to the tremendous forces of nature about them. An erupting volcano was a giant's heart, molten lava the giant's blood, his death an earthquake. It is part of the human urge to have an explanation for everything.

The Indian story is told of the hero Coyote, how he met an old woman who warned him about just walking around because he might meet a giant who kills everybody. Coyote told her giants didn't frighten him, even though he had never met one. He would kill the giant with ease.

The old woman warned Coyote, saying the giant was bigger and closer than he thought, but Coyote said he didn't care, that a giant would be about as big as a bull moose and that he could kill one easily. Continuing on his way he saw a large fallen branch and picked it up to use as a club. He was sure it would be big enough and heavy enough to kill a giant, and he walked on, whistling merrily, right into a huge cave in the middle of the path.

In the dark cave, Coyote met a woman crawling along on the ground, who upon

The giant's belly? Black Butte, Interstate 5, northern California.

seeing him said she was starving, was too weak to walk, and asked what he was doing with the stick.

Coyote replied that he was going to kill the giant with it and asked if the woman knew where the giant was hiding. Feeble as she was, the woman laughed and informed Coyote he was already deep within the giant's belly. He had already been eaten!

Coyote could not understand how he could be in the giant's belly, knowing very well that he hadn't even seen him. The woman told him that Coyote had probably thought it was a cave when he walked into his mouth. It was easy to walk in but nobody had ever walked out. This giant is so big, she said, that you can't see all of him. His belly fills a whole valley.

Throwing his stick away, Coyote kept on walking, not knowing what else to do, when he came across other people who had walked into the cave, all of them lying around half

dead and sick. They said they were starving to death, trapped inside the giant.

Coyote realized that if they were really inside the giant, then the cave walls must be the inside of his stomach, and they decided to cut out some meat from the giant. Using his hunting knife, he cut chunks out of the cave walls, finding they were indeed the giant's fat and meat, and fed the starving people. He even went back and gave some to the starving woman he had first met.

Everyone imprisoned in the giant's belly soon felt stronger and happier, but not completely so, because they could think of no way to escape their prison in the belly.

Coyote told them not to worry, saying he would kill the giant by stabbing him in the heart. He couldn't find the heart until someone thought of looking at the distant volcano puffing and beating. Coyote was sure the volcano was the heart and began to slash away at the mountain, until the giant com-

plained, telling him to stop stabbing and cutting and to leave him alone. The giant said everyone could leave, that if they would stop the disturbance in his stomach, he would open his mouth.

Coyote was not yet ready to leave, and he continued hacking at the heart. Telling the others to get ready, he explained that as the giant died there would be an earthquake and that when the giant opened his jaws to take a last breath, they should run out fast since he would then close his mouth tightly, forever.

A deep hole was cut in the giant's heart, and molten lava started to flow out like an eruption. It was the giant's blood. The giant groaned and the ground under the people's feet trembled as the mouth opened and the people ran out.

The last one out was the wood tick, and he almost didn't make it as the giant's teeth closed upon him. Coyote managed to pull him through at the last moment, but the wood tick was squeezed by the giant's teeth, which is why the wood tick is always flat.

VOLCANIC ACTIVITY HAS ALWAYS PROVIDED appropriate linguistic devices for early peoples to explain the unknown. Homer used the same in his epic tale of Ulysses, when Circe sent Ulysses to visit the Halls of Hades on the River Pyriphlegethon, the river of flaming fire, and Cocytus, the river of lamentation. Historical events are often related to eruptions. Narcisse Achille, Comte de Salvandy, made the apt comparison when at a *fête* given by the Duc d'Orleans for the King of Naples during the French Revolution, he commented, "We are dancing on a volcano." Havelock Ellis adds, "All civilization has from time to time become a thin crust over a volcano of revolution." The volcano allegory, a comparison of real life to the unimaginable, is a common invention of writers embroidering an otherwise ordinary phrase. As Lord Byron wrote, poetry is "the lava of the imagination whose eruption prevents an earthquake." Shelley noted, "With hue like that when some great painter dips his pencil in the gloom of earthquake and eclipse."

In the *Journal of Irreproducible Results*, a parody of scientific papers, a last scientific word on the real causes of continental drift and earthquakes is an article authored by biochemist George Kaub, arguing that the North American continent faces the likelihood of sinking into the sea because *National Geographic* magazine subscribers like to keep their heavy publication, never throw any away, and store every copy in attics, spare rooms, and garages. The magazines never disappear—they are given to someone else or passed on to their children. As a result, Kaub predicts, the cumulative weight will compress until they become plastic and begin to flow like molten magma. Fissures will appear in the earth, and buildings, towns and entire cities will tumble into them. He says, "Affluent areas of high subscription density will be the first to go." Warning of this dire end, Kaub contends the increased earthquake activity along the San Andreas fault is not only because many easterners are moving west to the Sunbelt, but "most are bringing their *Geographics* with them!"

We may not be able to actually predict volcanoes and earthquakes or know what they mean, but there is no dearth of wise and perceptive conjecture.

Kilauea east rift erupts in field of Vanda orchids, Puna, Hawaii.

CHAPTER TEN

The Shaking Future Earth

Golden Gate Bridge, California.

The continent shakes and moves. Southern California and coastal lands south of San Francisco slip in jerks past the rest of California at a rate averaging 2.6 inches per year; the Atlantic Ocean spreads 0.6 inches per year. South America continues drifting away from Africa at about 2 inches per year, and Hawaii still creeps toward Siberia at about the same rate. The Pacific Ocean grows wider by about ½ inch per year and basin-and-range country— the Sierra, Tetons, and Rockies—continue to be squeezed and deformed as northern and southern edges of the Pacific plate push beneath the North American continent. The Pacific Northwest rumbles as a mountain explodes, and falling ash quietly drifts onto farmlands of western states first covered by ash from an erupting Mt. Mazama thousands of years ago. Central California shakes as magma again nears the surface where lava last burst forth only 600 years ago.

Like the Hawaiian Islands, Yellowstone National Park drifts over a hot spot in the earth's mantle, a hot spot probably located off the Oregon coast 65 million years ago, a trail marked by a path of volcanic vents, lava flows, and giant cracks extending across Oregon, Idaho, and Wyoming. The geology is quite evident in Boise where downtown offices and homes on Warm Springs Avenue are today still heated by 170° Fahrenheit water obtained from drilled wells below the city. It's been a working geothermal system for almost 100 years. A catastrophic eruption has occurred in Yellowstone about every 600,000 years, and another eruption in the ancient caldera, today covered by puffing geysers and Yellowstone Lake, is about due; the caldera floor within the national park continues to rise.

South of Yellowstone our unstable planet reveals even more fragility where stresses are breaking apart New Mexico in a giant crack along the great Rio Grande rift, perhaps six times deeper than the Grand Canyon. Now filled largely with old lava and river sediment, it, too, is growing a bit wider each year. Scott Baldridge of nearby Los Alamos National Laboratory describes the crack as "a hell of a hole." Most residents of Santa Fe and Albuquerque are doubtless unaware they actually live astride what may be the deepest and longest crack in the planet's wrinkled crust east of the San Andreas.

It is still quite hot under the western basin-and-range states as aging segments of the Pacific plate slip farther beneath the continent, heating the subsurface mantle and remelting rocks squishing through cracks extending closer and closer to the surface crust. The land stretches and thins out, dropping valley basins and pushing up old mountains.

Salt Lake City was some 200 to 300 miles closer to Reno 15 million years ago. Today they continue pulling apart as small faults spread stresses around, pushing up hills and dropping new scarps. Jarring, noticeable earthquakes are unusual in the Midwest, but the 1959 Montana quake at Hebgen Lake, were 29 campers were buried in a landslide, and the 7.3 shock near Challis, Idaho, in 1983, where a collapsing brick storefront killed 2 pedestrians, are evidence of rare and poorly understood events. The dramatic mountain backdrop for Salt Lake City, the Wasatch Range, is a gigantic escarpment not unlike the eastern side of the Sierra where faults do not subside gently.

California's Long Valley caldera, today containing Mammoth Lakes Resort and 25,000 skiers on winter weekends, in geologic yesterdays long ago dropped volcanic ash on Atlantic coast states. Swarms of harmonic vibrations, most unfelt on the surface, are regularly measured beneath the caldera floor by sensitive instruments for scientists to plot movement of magma slowly creeping upward toward the surface, spreading apart cracks in ancient rock. The magma is only 3.5 miles beneath the surface today.

Columnar basalt, Devil's Postpile National Monument, California.

In northern California earthquakes remind those living in the shadow of Mt. Shasta, presently quiet in its mantle of winter snow, that Mt. St. Helens farther north in the Cascade Range had been silent for over a century before blowing apart seven days after the first strong quake in 123 years. All Cascade volcanoes are considered active—Mt. Rainier, Mt. Shasta, Mt. Hood, even Crater Lake are all capable of erupting again. Some volcanologists give the nod to the Three Sisters area west of Bend, Oregon, as the most probable site of renewed volcanic activity in the Pacific Northwest.

Mt. St. Augustine in Alaska erupts once a year while Hawaii's Kilauea volcano spits lava once a month, assuring its place in scientific record books as one of the most active volcano in the world. The earth remains hot inside, churning the earth's molten core and forcing continental and oceanic segments of the crust together and apart. It will continue in this manner until the sun inevitably expands and incinerates the earth. There will be an estimated five billion more years of earthquakes and volcanoes until all is finally quiet.

At any moment a powerful earthquake generated by slippage along the San Andreas fault may strike Los Angeles, the most threatened city in the United States. Scientists agree that sometime within the next 14 years or so a great earthquake is likely to deliver a destructive blow to southern California cities. A violent quake possibly measuring upward of 8.3 on the Richter scale, equal to the explosive fury of 200 million tons of TNT, could occur tomorrow. A quake of the same force occurred in San Francisco in 1906.

As many as 30,000 people could be killed. Another 100,000 would need hospitalization. Thousands of older buildings in the central urban area would simply collapse into piles of brick, burying occupants. Should the shock occur during the day, as many as 2,000 students at the University of California in Los Angeles could die in the many collapsing, unreinforced campus buildings. There would be perhaps $60 billion of property destroyed. The economy would come to a lurching halt.

Glass from downtown office towers would shower pedestrians with deadly shards as chemical storage tanks thoughout the area split open to release all kinds of easily ignited toxic chemicals, feeding fires difficult to extinguish as broken water mains emptied storage reservoirs not to be filled again for weeks. Aqueducts carrying water from northern California and Owens Valley would be broken in a dozen places along the fault line.

Potential physical destruction depends a lot on soil conditions, proximity of quake epicenter to urban structures, and time of day. Homeward-bound commuter traffic would be severely dislocated, and failure of only a few overpass structures would immediately transform Los Angeles basin freeways into parking lots, forcing traffic onto earthquake-littered surface streets. Within minutes, perhaps 250,000 would be homeless, apartments and condos blazing into ruin. If the quake occurred late in the afternoon during the homeward-bound rush, the worst possible time, fatalities could easily exceed 40,000, and few of the thousands seriously injured would be able to find a hospital to treat them. With the the quake occurring during business hours, considerable emotional strain would result from separation of family members—parents from each other and children at school, coupled with the unknown consequences of thousands missing; others trapped on destroyed freeway interchanges, in traffic jams, and in shattered buildings. Worst of all would be the concern for those lost between school and home and the last telephone call. "If we had a devastating quake, it can be assumed there will be points that will exhaust our resources," warns the Los Angeles Police Department. "For the first three days . . . the people of this city are going to have to take care of themselves."

A shock even less powerful than the one that devastated Mexico City in 1985 could rupture hundreds of chemical and fuel storage tanks, igniting fireballs, releasing poisonous gases, and fueling the conflagration of adjacent oil refineries. Southern California residents would be exposed to fumes as deadly as those that swept over Bhopal, India, killing more than 2,000 people after an industrial chemical leak. Many more than the number of victims in Bhopal would be counted in a catastrophic shock rupturing only 10 percent of the chemical tanks in the El Segundo-Long Beach industrial corridors, where 15,000 residents in the immediate area would breathe a life-threatening toxic cloud.

Kilauea Iki cinder cone. The Ohia lehua tree has been stripped of bark by hot cinder fallout. Hawaii Volcanoes National Park.

Downtown Los Angeles, on the edge of the moving Pacific plate, California.

With freeways in gridlock, there would be no way to escape. Over a million people would be affected by deadly fumes in the densely populated region extending from the south bay harbor to northern and western Orange County. Everyone would be exposed, and unless they were evacuated quickly the toxic fumes would be strong enough to kill or cause long-term serious health problems. No matter what advance earthquake preparations are undertaken, and Orange County is better prepared than most, a major disaster would occur.

Officials of emergency management planning for the Orange County Fire Department say planning for an earthquake with these consequences is impossible. "It would cost so much money that it would be impractical to deal with it." Major petrochemical industries in southern California store as much as 540 tons of chlorine, a chemical just as deadly

as the gas in Bhopal, where no more than 90 tons of methyl isocyanate were released. The cost to retrofit chemical companies with earthquake-resistant systems and keep emergency workers and repair facilities on permanent standby would be in the billions of dollars. The communities involved simply do not have the funds to prevent catastrophe, nor could they assemble enough resources quickly enough during a major earthquake to break up the deadly clouds.

Abandoned and active oil fields would also pose problems when sheared-off oil well shafts release flammable methane gas. Many of the Los Angeles basin's most concentrated residential and business areas have been built on abandoned oil and gas fields. There are 70 oil fields with thousands of old wells littering Los Angeles and Orange counties, almost all surrounded and covered by uncounted numbers of urban developments. Improperly

Overleaf: Napa Valley vineyards in volcanic soil, California.

abandoned oil wells will cause paved streets to erupt in flame, joining the 480 miles of underground fuel lines and ruptured natural-gas mains in a general conflagration even Hollywood has not imagined.

The last day for Los Angeles and Orange County would have begun like any other—a foggy summer morning changing to smoggy sunshine by midday, jammed freeways clogging traffic on surface streets, immigrant workers pushing clothing through sewing machines in the garment district while others washed the glass walls on the downtown Bonaventure Hotel.

At Huntington Beach, surfers would test early morning waves while night fishermen walk off the Santa Monica Beach pier with a lucky catch. Disneyland's parking lot would fill with tourists anxious to experience Michael Jackson's Captain EO. Sherilyn Mentes would prepare her Hawaii film for an afternoon showing in Azusa. Mentes's home in San Clemente already displays ceiling cracks from previous gentle quakes, part of the southern California environment that is casually accepted no less than windstorms in Kansas and hail in Omaha.

A low rumble would be heard first, seeming to emanate from nowhere and everywhere, a gentle rocking alerting residents to the unnatural, frightening movement of the rocky earth beneath. Dogs would bark, windows rattle, and buildings creak. Drivers on the freeways would feel nothing until they became aware of swaying light poles and vibrating directional signs.

The ground would shake. And shake. The heaving would increase until it was impossible to stand as bookcases tore away from walls, dishes and pans smashed together on kitchen floors. Downtown office towers would sway, throwing computers to the floor as windows shattered, spraying glass into the eyes of anyone daring to look. Panic and terror would take over as uncontrollable shaking increased with catastrophic intensity within minutes. Realization of the long-expected calamity and the hope of survival are the inevitable fate of Californians—the fate of people who insist on building cities upon the west's most restless and unstable real estate.

Experts writing in the earthquake response plan published by California's Office of Emergency Services assert, "A disaster of this

magnitude within the confines of the United States is unprecedented since the Civil War."

The United States Geological Survey (USGS) in Menlo Park offers no assurance of any less. Bill Ellsworth, chief of the seismology branch, says, "We know that the great earthquake will come. The question is when." The 26 million inhabitants of California are not able to escape their fragile geology. They live by desire astride the moving San Andreas fault.

It is ironic that many of the desirable features making southern California an attractive place to live are the result of major geologic movement long before the first orange growers arrived, thousands of years before even local Indians settled in the warm desert basin. It is understood as fact that if Californians voted on the issue, they would accept the risks of moving faults rather than move onto dull flatlands east of the shaking state. Californians await disaster by preparing for it—a little. But whether residents are actually prepared to handle an 8.3 is still unknown. As a Pacific Bell spokesman quoted in the Los Angeles Times put it, "No amount of anything we've been doing would help us if we were leveled." The impact of such a quake is almost incomprehensible.

Californians must adapt to the threat, whether they live in Los Angeles or San Francisco, where San Andreas will shake them, or in the volcanically hazardous Sierra resort at Mammoth Lakes or farther north in Weed at the foot of the Mt. Shasta volcano. Residents acknowledge the danger, but most compare it to the risk of any natural disaster. "Anywhere you live in the world you are going to encounter natural hazards," said Ellsworth. "In the West we have earthquakes."

Longtime football fans attending games at the University of California at Berkeley are well aware that Memorial Stadium is considered an earthquake risk. An active trace of the Hayward fault runs through the entire length of the stadium, and separation of the concrete sections can be clearly seen where geological fault creep is slowly pulling the stadium apart. Have no fear, however, as this has never been viewed by university administrators as a great threat to life, since the stadium, which has a capacity of 75,662 is totally filled for only six afternoon games per year. Some California alumni may actually wish there was a fault slip during the annual

San Francisco, on the edge of the Continental plate.

altercation with Stanford, the institution across the bay in Palo Alto with a campus that was damaged during the 1906 quake.

Most Californians expect a major quake, but are satisfied they personally will escape injury. A statewide poll in California found that 62 percent felt they would be at risk from a large quake, but only 11 percent said they have serious concerns about the problem, and half of those respondents said they never worry. The human tendency is to assume injury will always happen to someone else, and Californians are no exception.

Federal Emergency Management people have developed considerable data about what the agency describes as "expectable" major California earthquakes. In the order of their expected Richter magnitude, they follow:

8.3 Los Angeles-San Bernardino on the San Andreas fault

8.3 San Francisco Bay area on the San Andreas fault

7.5 Los Angeles on the Newport-Inglewood fault

7.4 San Francisco Bay area on the Hayward fault

7.0 San Diego on the Rose Canyon fault

6.8 Riverside-San Bernardino on the Cucamonga fault

6.7 Los Angeles on the Santa Monica fault

Chances of major earthquakes caused by movement on the dangerous San Andreas and Hayward faults occurring in any year are two to five percent. Chances of serious earthquakes in the next 20 to 30 years are high in areas adjacent to the southern section of San Andreas, moderate on the northern sections of Hayward and Newport-Inglewood faults. On other faults the chances are low, but earthquakes will occur.

A catastrophic quake on the San Andreas fault will probably not come as a surprise. According to the Southern California Earth-

Mt. Augustine, Cook Inlet region, Alaska. Photo by Steve Kaufman.

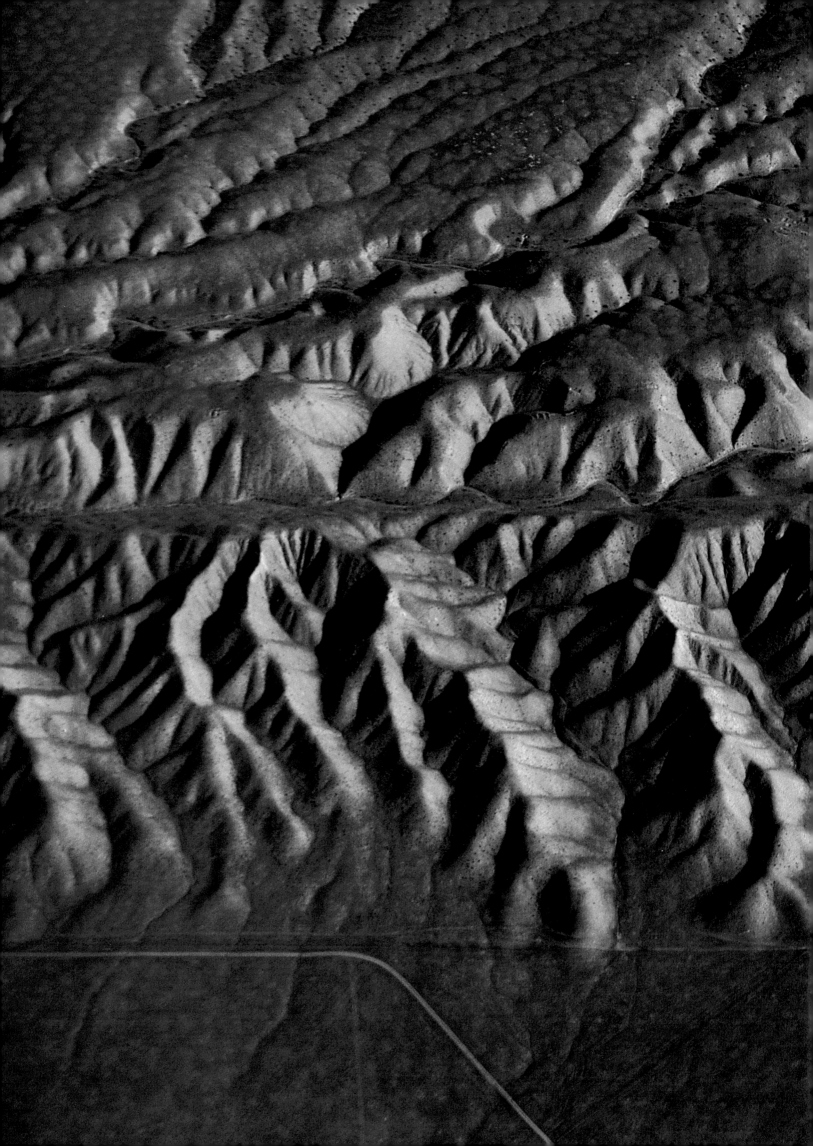

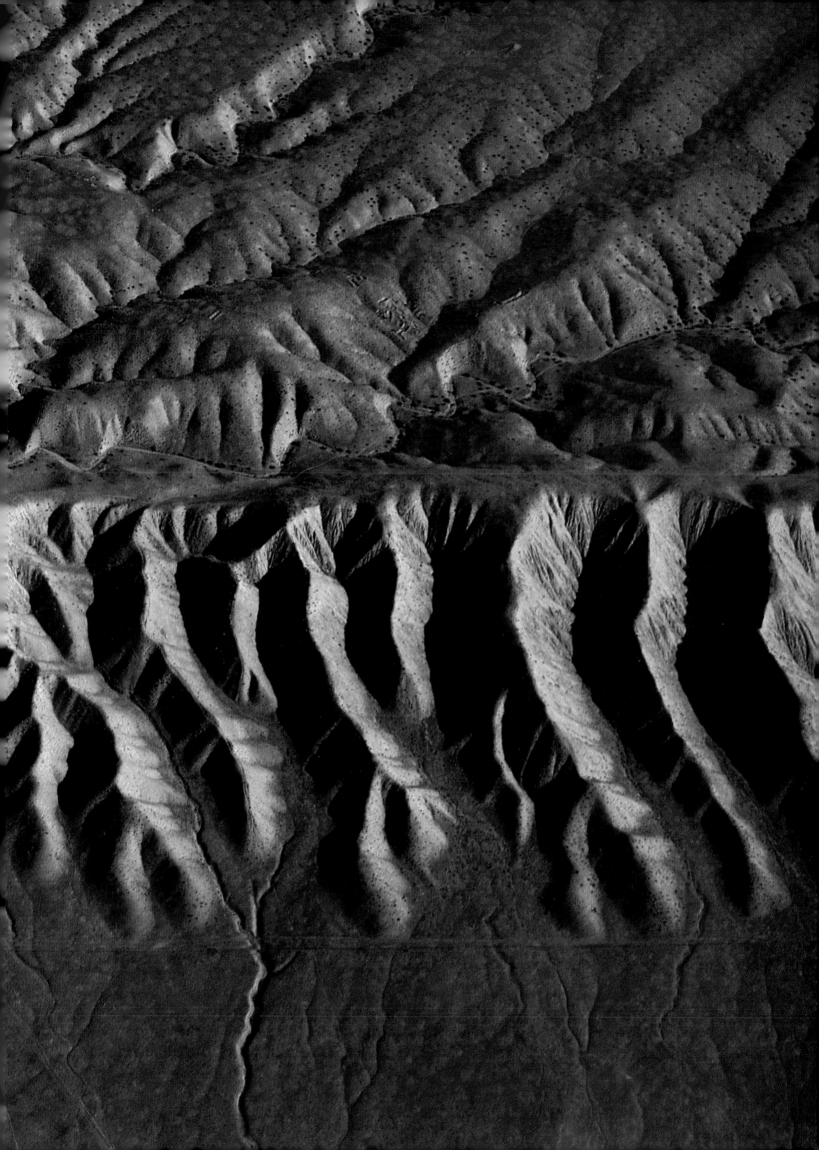

Homes in Daly City, California are astride the San Andreas Fault.

quake Preparedness Project, launched in the aftermath of the Mt. St. Helens eruption, there undoubtedly would be many warning signals—probably in the form of a series of minor shocks that would allow scientists to predict various possibilities over a week or so, but not a precise date or time, a difficulty that is becoming increasingly part of the problem. It could result in a whole new concern, including mass hysteria and panic following a warning or tentative prediction.

Earthquake preparedness does not extend to California hospitals, where as many as 93 percent do not meet earthquake safety standards established in a 13-year-old law. Even if billions of dollars were available to reinforce and rebuild older structures, the work by some estimates could not be completed before the year 2000 and might not be done until 2030, long after the expected major

quake had done its damage. The only action taken by the current state legislators is to study the matter again.

In the wake of a disastrous earthquake, residents may find it virtually impossible to telephone anyone, not because their telephone system is damaged but simply because too many people are trying to place calls at the same time. During a recent Richter 6 quake in the San Francisco South Bay area, three small businesses almost burned to the ground when a local fire station two miles away could not be reached by telephone. Bystanders took 15 minutes to drive to the firehouse and report the fire, started when a natural-gas line bringing fuel to a cleaning machine was severed by heavy shaking. Sparks from the machine ignited the gas in a microcosm of incidents expected to occur a hundred times over in major quakes.

Overleaf: San Andreas Fault, Carrizo Plain, southern California.

Some businessmen might prefer they be surprised by a destructive quake, not having the slightest idea of how to cope, much less contemplate the expense of adequate preparation. And to base even inadequate planning on the assumption that quakes will announce their approach may prove counterproductive, as effective preparation must be based on the accurate measure of potential destruction and probable location of the areas to be most heavily damaged: which buildings will collapse, which freeway overpasses will shift off their foundations and be closed, which railroad tracks will be twisted out of use, which airports will still be in use, what residential areas will be ordered evacuated when toxic chemicals are released.

As a planner with the Federal Emergency Management office expressed it, "We need to know what hospitals are going to go down. We need to be more site-specific." Yet this very information is impossible to catalog when advance notice of dates and magnitude cannot be predicted with any accuracy. It is all quite reasonable to inform the general public to stand in the doorway to be better protected from falling ceiling plaster, but there can be no realistic preparedness to protect the population from near total destruction. As a state senate aide commented, major quake preparedness legislation "was never sexy enough to get passed." Earthquakes are not a hot item unless an earthquake happens.

Scattered throughout the state are some 50,000 to 60,000 unreinforced masonry buildings, mostly built before enhanced structural codes were adopted after the 1933 Long Beach shake. A 1981 seismic survey of 1,350 state office buildings rated 250 as "poor" or "very poor," meaning they would not be standing after a major shock. It is estimated several billion dollars will be required to bring them up to code. The problem is so beyond anyone's ability to solve that most throw up

Rescue workers in Mexico City after the September 19, 1985 earthquake. Photo by Frances Stoppelman.

their hands and do nothing. It was not until the Mexico City earthquake and Colombia's volcano erupted and buried 25,000 people alive that state legislators began considering a sheaf of seismic bills to overcome bureaucratic sluggishness and concerns about legal liability.

Legal concerns pose a paradox voiced by opponents of state legislation requiring cities and counties to inventory seismically hazardous buildings that structural engineers claim will not withstand a major quake. Where these buildings are used by the public, identification as hazardous could destroy their business before the earthquake arrives, and for the city to know where they are and do nothing is to make the city liable when they fall down. It is a dilemma for legal counsel. Considering mounting deep-pocket liability problems already draining city coffers, it is understandable that few municipalities are taking earthquake preparedness seriously when preparedness means identifying and fixing buildings.

It has been suggested that the greatest risk from accurate prediction of an impending earthquake or volcanic eruption would be the probability of being trampled by tourists running into the area to photograph and personally witness the once-in-a-lifetime event. Should a forthcoming earthquake be announced during the afternoon at Disneyland or Knotts Berry Farm, it is debatable how many would abandon the park, having already purchased unlimited ride tickets for the day.

It may also be, in the present litigious environment, that, from a scientist's point of view, predicting an earthquake or volcanic eruption and not having it occur may be worse than a prediction that proves accurate. Giving a definite time and date prediction for a repeat of the 1906 shock in San Francisco could very well precipitate an evacuation and shutdown of the city horrendous to contemplate. Deaths on overcrowded freeways, traffic gridlocks of residents and tourists with no home for the night beyond Oakland, and halting of all business activity and banking, even for 24 hours, would result in liability claims beyond comprehension—if no earthquake then happened. If the quake did occur on schedule, the savings in lives would be considerable, however, even when property losses might require San Francisco to again start over. No lawsuits would then occur,

since by legal definition only God would be at fault.

San Francisco does not have the dangerous mix of office towers, residential communities, chemical industries, oil fields, and the easily damaged freeway system that spread over 2,000 square miles of the Los Angeles basin. Areas most susceptible to extensive damage in the bay area are on filled, reclaimed land along the waterfront and south on the peninsula. Daly City and Pacifica, directly astride San Andreas, will be split asunder, and all communities bordering the fault in the continuing megatropolis extending through famed Silicon Valley and beyond to San Jose and Morgan Hill can also expect to suffer.

A problem limited to the San Francisco Bay Area is the sixteen laboratories, corporations, and military facilities licensed to handle radioactive materials, facilities that could cause significant radioactive contamination following a major earthquake. Five especially vulnerable to seismic upheaval are in Alameda County, 40 miles east of San Francisco, location of the active Hayward and Calaveras faults and the recently discovered east-west oriented Las Positas fault. With the potential of causing an earthquake measuring up to Richter 7.5, movement of these secondary faults could be triggered by sudden slippage on nearby San Andreas, resulting in simultaneous disruption of public services and radioactive leases in the Bay Area.

Largest of the East Bay facilities is the Lawrence Livermore Laboratory, where advanced nuclear weapons systems are designed and constructed. For this purpose the laboratory maintains at its site a large inventory of plutonium, fluctuating from 600 to 800 pounds. Some of the plutonium is flown in from Rocky Flats in Colorado, some trucked in from Hanford military reactors in Washington state, and smaller quantities are manufactured in Livermore's own on-site reactor.

Shifting faults in the immediate vicinity of the site could break open storage containers and contaminate several reservoirs and aqueducts bordering Livermore Valley that supply drinking water to millions of people in San Francisco and South Bay cities. According to *Not Man Apart*, state and county earthquake code inspectors have never been permitted to investigate the reactors and research labs at Livermore because the

Atomic Energy Commission and its successor, the Nuclear Regulatory Commission, have preempted inspection powers.

As a whole, California homeowners are definitely bucking the odds on earthquake insurance. They are generally uninterested. Earthquake damage policies have been available in the state since the 1920s, but only 1 homeowner in 20 has bought the coverage. It isn't cheap if the house is close to a seismically active fault, and where it's far away and affordable, residents with a devil-may-care approach to shaking insurance are betting that even if a big quake hits, damage to most homes will be zero or close to it. Others may calculate that it will be cheaper in the long run to obtain inexpensive federal disaster loans after the quake, when often the government doesn't require repayment of the first $2,500 loaned. It's sort of a $2,500 deductible in reverse.

Banks and savings and loan associations are apparently not worried. Security Pacific National Bank has over $4.5 billion in loans spread around the state and does not require mortgagees to purchase earthquake insurance as it does for fire coverage. After all, there has never been an earthquake that affected all the state, and when quakes have occurred, they've always been limited to local areas.

"Our loans in San Francisco are going to be OK if some part of Los Angeles is hit," says Monroe Morgan, senior vice president of Great Western Financial Corporation, California's third-largest savings and loan association. It so happens that Great Western doesn't even insure its own Beverly Hills tower headquarters against earthquakes, although the company has signed for coverage of a low-rise computer center in the San Fernando Valley where soil conditions indicate even a moderate quake would be very destructive.

A 1906 San Francisco-style quake would without doubt have a serious adverse affect on any money institution headquartered in San Francisco, because of computer damage, employee injuries, and the obvious impossibility of workers to even get to the office in shattered highrises. A San Francisco bank operations officer agrees that a serious quake would be a "tremendous" problem, but losses on the bank's multimillion-dollar mortgage portfolio? "That's not our concern," was the reply. A major fire engulfing a large part of Los Angeles following the predicted "big one," would have similar consequences affecting every financial and insurance organization in the state.

If insurance companies had to pay for residential earthquake damage even though homeowners didn't have quake insurance, as recent state court decisions have affirmed by saying the blame could be laid on other factors, such as shoddy contractor's workmanship, insurers would be unable to pay the enormous claims following a major earthquake. "The reserves built up by insurance companies would be wiped out overnight," asserted Vic Slavin, vice president of the American Insurance Association. "No one will collect anything because we'll be broke."

Most fire insurance policies at the time of the 1906 San Francisco fire and earthquake had an exemption from earthquake damage, so thousands of property owners, in order to collect on their insurance, claimed that their buildings did not collapse during the quake, but were destroyed by fire afterwards. Much of San Francisco may have been rebuilt on fraud.

Many earthquake-preparedness programs sponsored by governmental agencies will be revealed as quite inadequate when the predicted large quake actually occurs. On the fringes of the epicenter, common-sense preparedness will undoubtedly prevent many injuries, even death, and enable survivors to live on their own resources for weeks without gas, water, and electricity, as long as they still have a roof on the house—preparedness such as bolting bookcases to the wall, storing china in closed kitchen cabinets, having a gas meter shut-off wrench handy, full water storage bottles, replacing glass with acrylic in picture frames, strapping water heaters to the wall, and storing boxes of diapers for medical emergencies. A medical kit and how-to medical book, dehydrated food, and dog or cat food may be required as will storing all the other items that will no longer be available for purchase at the supermarket. Batteries for flashlights, portable radios, and children's toys will be needed, as well as spare prescription eyeglasses, medication for next month, tools, and comfortable walking shoes for when the car cannot be driven down streets filled with rubble.

Business is booming for California survival companies selling to homeowners and corporations bracing for the quake. An $85 home inspection is offered by the Earthquake Safety Organization, a company in Palo Alto prepared to tell anyone how to prepare for one of nature's most lethal phenomena. Other companies are Redi, Inc., Creative Home Economics Services, Hearthwatch, Quake Safe, and Epi-Center, a firm selling specially constructed plastic "earthquake-resistant" water storage bottles, priced from $12.50 to $27.50, depending on how much you expect to drink.

Epi-Center programs on earthquake preparedness are sponsored by cities that guarantee sales quotas for plastic bottles and earthquake intensity maps sold at the seminars. The intensity maps are said by the company to be a particularly "hot" item for Christmas giving. Cities are clamoring to participate, regardless of the obvious commercialization of earthquakes, because tight municipal funding resulting from California's Proposition 13 limiting property taxes has made it difficult for cities to finance their own earthquake safety programs. For a fee of $2,400, corporations can have an Epi-Center geologist inform them how close they are to a fault line and the degree of projected earthquake intensity to be expected when the fault moves.

Shaking up earthquake complacency is a continuing challenge for Pacific Coast communities; many have joined with private survival companies to alert residents to prepare for disaster. Yet the coming earthquake is not a subject people like to think about or worry over. The image of your home breaking apart, your best crystal tumbling out of cupboards and smashing on the floor, children screaming and dogs barking, and your life's savings—everything your home represents in the way of memories and love—about to be lost forever is not the image people can dwell on for very long.

Following the first tragic days, even the best organized, most redundant medical facilities will be simply overwhelmed by the enormous number of casualties. Helicopters will be the only realistic way of transporting the injured, since paramedic vehicles will be unable to move far on impassable streets. Improvised medical facilities in neighborhood schools and hotel lobbies, filled with the few doctors and nurses still alive, will be forced to make heartbreaking choices as they treat to the best of their ability with limited

medical supplies and equipment only those most likely to survive.

Self-sufficiency is the rule for survival in any natural disaster. In the aftermath of the 8.3 earthquake, entire communities will be cut off from outside help, and demand for emergency services will overwhelm local government. Mobilization of state and federal agencies will take days or weeks, if anything is left to mobilize. It is estimated that in San Francisco, 7,000 out of 8,000 hospital beds would be destroyed or unusable, along with medication and surgical supplies. Preparedness is meaningless when it involves medical treatment of 40,000 people in a city with totally insufficient medical resources and blood-bank reserves, resources that have been destroyed.

Residents beyond the area of serious damage, far enough from the epicenter to escape widespread devastation, perhaps experiencing only nervous shaking and cracked ceilings, will be engulfed by survivors who lost everything but their lives. Looting will be an ever-present danger in damaged districts, and those who did prepare in advance with stocks of food and water may find it necessary to defend themselves, without police help, from foraging bands of the hungry and homeless. Driving to another city after the quake to escape chaos will not be easy, even if one is willing to abandon property. Most freeways will be blocked by fallen overpasses and accidents. Debris on surface streets and remains of fallen buildings will make driving dangerous, and even where roads are found to be open there is a risk because nobody will have reliable information on how far the road is passable, or if gas can be found. The AAA will not be available to start your car.

MORE THAN 20,000 EARTHQUAKES are recorded every year in California. Most are too weak to be noticed—none have been predicted. Numerous earthquake advisories have been issued by the USGS and state emergency offices. No earthquakes warned of in advisories have occurred. There has been one successful prediction of volcanic eruption by the USGS, Mt. St. Helens in May 1980, although the prediction was far from perfect, lacking as it did a short-term warning, but the knowledge of impending disaster doubtless reduced loss of life in the popular forest

The Windy Ridge forest was flattened by the exploding volcano, Mt. St. Helens National Monument, Washington.

and recreational region. USGS spokesmen say their advisories are warnings, issued to make the public aware of the necessity of being prepared—they are not predictions. The advisory "doesn't mean there's going to be an earthquake—it's just your risk is up a bit."

Experts agree, however, that sometime within the next 14 years a great earthquake will deliver a massive knockout punch to Los Angeles. Considering the present status of earthquake prediction, the shock will strike without warning, at any time. It is not a question of if but when the earthquake will arrive to shake our lives apart.

Scientists may be unwilling to issue a warning, for the costs of a false word—unnecessary evacuation and panic—are potentially great. Residents will be understandably reluctant to respond—their businesses, schools, homelife, and future would be disrupted, perhaps permanently—and just

as we take our chances on the freeway every day, it would be easier to stay at home and take our chances. Even at Mt. St. Helens, where it was clearly evident that an eruption might occur, everyone did not leave. Yet the potential cataclysmic consequences of an 8.3 quake centered in an urban area justify reasonable efforts to prepare for the unimaginable, even while the unpredicted is easier to ignore.

CENTURIES AGO, THERE WERE orderly rows of corn and pepper growing on the lower slopes of Cerro Gordo in Mexico. Children grazed goats on the grassy foothills while their mothers carded wool in the shade of the largest trees. At the base of the mountain a busy city marketplace invited merchants and travelers from distant trading centers to exchange products and philosophy. Teoti-

Popocatepetl, Chalco, Mexico.

huacán was the largest city in Mesoamerica—a place of great beauty with broad avenues, thousands of apartments for residents, impressive pyramids and temples. The city was located in a valley surrounded by volcanic peaks generating weather for water and obsidian for weapons. The volcanoes were worshipped, not feared.

Without warning, as evidenced by archaeological investigations, the volcano erupted, set fire to the city, and buried it, destroying the Teotihuacan civilization. Today only a museum shows the city's past glory while the volcanoes, extinct for a thousand years, remain quiet.

Another cataclysm now waits to happen, but it is too enormous a calamity to believe. The priests probably did not warn the Teotihuacan citizens of the probability of an eruption that would destroy them. It would have destroyed their credibility. Scientists tell us that some places we have chosen to build and live on, because they're warm and where crops grow well or there is a safe harbor, are not necessarily the safest of places, although we cleared the land and built the first house without asking why the earth was cracked and mountains hot. It was enough that the oranges grew. We cannot accept that the earth beneath us can destroy us.

There is the chance that a nuclear power plant will leak. There is a chance that we will be struck by a shooting star and the earth will warm up or cool down, freeze in a new ice age, or melt the polar glaciers and flood our coastal cities. The list of possible natural calamities is long, and while we depict them in movies and novels and write books about our possible misfortunes, few believe they will ever happen. Impossible events we cannot accept. After all, we are only human. We'll take our chances.

Bibliography

Achad, Frater. *Ancient Mystical White Brotherhood.* Phoenix: Great Seal Press, 1976.

Allen, John Eliot. *The Magnificent Gateway.* Forest Grove, OR: Timber Press, 1984.

Alt, David D. and Hyundman, Donald W. *Roadside Geology of Oregon.* Missoula: Mountain Press, 1978.

——— . *Roadside Geology of Washington.* Missoula: Mountain Press, 1984.

——— . *Roadside Geology of Northern California.* Missoula: Mountain Press, 1975.

——— . *Roadside Geology of the Northern Rockies.* Missoula: Mountain Press, 1972.

Aslett, Jim. *Lava Beds Underground.* Klamath Falls: Lava Beds Natural History Association, 1982.

Blackstone, D.L., Jr. *Traveler's Guide to the Geology of Wyoming.* Laramie: Geological Survey of Wyoming, 1971.

Blair, M.L.; Spangle, W.E.; Spangle, William; and Associates. *Seismic Safety and Land-Use Planning—Selected Examples from California.* Washington, DC: Geological Survey Professional Paper 941-B, 1979.

Bolt, Bruce A. *Earthquakes and Volcanoes.* San Francisco: W.H. Freeman, 1951–1980.

Borcherdt, R.D. *Studies for Seismic Zonation of the San Francisco Bay Region.* Washington, DC: Geological Survey Professional Paper 941-A, 1979.

Brogan, Phil F. *East of the Cascades.* Portland, OR: Binford & Mort, 1977.

Brundage, Burr Cartwright. *The Fifth Sun: Aztec Gods, Aztec World.* Austin: University of Texas Press, 1979.

Carlson, Loraine. *Mexico City.* Chicago: Upland Press, 1981.

——— . *Yucatan.* Chicago: Upland Press, 1982.

——— . *Guatemala.* Chicago: Upland Press, 1981.

Cere, James M. and Shah, Haresh C. *Terra Non Firma: Understanding and Preparing for Earthquakes.* New York: W.H. Freeman, 1984.

Cerve, W.S. *Lemuria: The Lost Continent of the Pacific.* San Jose, CA: Supreme Grand Lodge of AMORC, 1954.

Chronic, Halka. *Pages of Stone.* Seattle: The Mountaineers, 1984.

——— . *Roadside Geology of Colorado.* Missoula: Mountain Press, 1980.

——— . *Roadside Geology of Arizona.* Missoula: Mountain Press, 1983.

Clements, Thomas. *Geological Story of Death Valley.* Death Valley: Death Valley '49ers, 1982.

Coe, Michael D. *Mexico.* New York: Thames and Hudson, 1962.

Colby, William E., editor. *John Muir's Studies in the Sierra.* San Francisco: Sierra Club, 1960.

Crandell, Dwight R. *Recent Eruptive History of Mount Hood, Oregon, and Potential Hazards from Future Eruptions.* Washington, DC: Geological Survey Bulletin 1492, 1980.

——— . *Potential Hazards from Future Eruptions of Mount Rainier, Washington.* Washington, DC: USGS Miscellaneous Geologic Investigations Map I-836, 1973.

Cranson, K.R. *Crater Lake—Gem of the Cascades:* Lansing, MI: Lansing Community College, 1980.

Daily News and Journal-American. *Volcano: The Eruption of Mount St. Helens.* Longview, WA: Longview Publishing, 1980.

Decker, Robert and Decker, Barbara. *Volcanoes and the Earth's Interior.* San Francisco: W.H. Freeman, 1975–1982.

——— . *Volcano Watching.* Hawaii: Hawaii Natural History Association, 1980.

DeNevi, Don. *Earthquakes.* Millbrae, CA: Celestial Arts, 1977.

Ekman, Leonard C. *Scenic Geology of the Pacific Northwest.* Portland, OR: Binford & Mort, 1970.

Erdoes, Richard and Ortiz, Alfonso. *American Indian Myths and Legends.* New York: Pantheon Books, 1984.

Fischer, William A. *Earthquake! Yellowstone's Living Geology.* Yellowstone: Yellowstone Library and Museum Association, 1960.

Fritz, William J. *Roadside Geology of the Yellowstone Country.* Missoula: Mountain Press, 1985.

Frome, Michael. *Battle for the Wilderness.* New York: Praeger, 1974.

Gaines, David. *Mono Lake Guidebook.* Lee Vining: Kutsavi Books, 1981.

Galloway, Alan J. *Geology of the Point Reyes Peninsula.* Sacramento: California Division of Mines and Geology Bulletin 202, 1977.

Gribbin, John. *This Shaking Earth.* New York: G.P. Putnam's Sons, 1978.

Harbaugh, John W. *Northern California: Geology Field Guide.* Dubuque, IA: Kendall/Hunt, 1975.

Harris, Ann and Tuttle, Esther. *Geology of National Parks.* Dubuque, IA: Kendall/Hunt, 1977.

Harris, Stephen L. *Fire & Ice: The Cascade Volcanoes.* Seattle: The Mountaineers, 1980.

Hatton, Raymond R. *High Country of Central Oregon.* Portland, OR: Binford & Mort, 1980.

Hays, W.W. *Facing Geologic and Hydrologic Hazards.* Washington, DC: Geological Survey Professional Paper 1240-B, 1981.

Hill, Mary. *Geology of the Sierra Nevada.* Berkeley: University of California Press, 1975.

Holsinger, Rosemary. *Shasta Indian Tales.* Happy Camp, CA: Naturegraph Publishers, 1982.

Iacopi, Robert. *Earthquake Country.* Menlo Park: Sunset Books, 1976.

Instituto Nacional de Antropología e Historia. *Materiales Para La Arqueología de Teotihuacan.* Mexico, 1968.

Instituto Nacional de Antropología e Historia. *Teotihuacan 80–82.* Mexico, 1982.

Kammerer, Raymond C. *Old Mission San Juan Capistrano.* Cincinnati: K/M Communications, 1980.

Keefer, William R. *The Geologic Story of Yellowstone National Park.* Yellowstone: Yellowstone Library and Museum Association, 1976.

King, Godfre Ray. *Original Unveiled Mysteries.* Chicago: Saint Germain Press, 1982.

Love, J.D. and Reed, John C., Jr. *Creation of the Teton Landscape.* Moose, WY: Grand Teton Natural History Association, 1971.

MacDonald, Gordon A. and Abbott, Agatin. *Volcanoes in the Sea.* Honolulu: University of Hawaii Press, 1970.

———— and Hubbard, Douglas. *Volcanoes of the National Parks of Hawaii.* Hawaii: Hawaii National History Association, 1978.

McPhee, John. *Basin and Range.* New York: Farrar, Straus & Giroux, 1980.

Mather, Kirtley F. *The Earth Beneath Us.* New York: Random House, 1975.

Meyer, Karl E. *Teotihuacan.* New York: *Newsweek,* 1973.

Muir, John. *The Mountains of California.* New York: Doubleday & Company, 1961.

National Geographic Society. *Exploring Our Living Planet.* Washington, DC: 1983.

Nations, Dale and Stump, Edmund. *Geology of Arizona.* Dubuque, IA: Kendall/Hunt, 1981.

Nichols, D.R. and Buchanan-Banks, J.M. *Seismic Hazards and Land-Use Planning.* Washington, DC: Geological Survey Circular 690, 1974.

Oakeshott, Gordon B. *California's Changing Landscapes.* San Francisco and New York: McGraw-Hill, 1971.

Pattison, Ken. *Milestones on Vancouver Island.* Victoria, British Columbia: Pattison Ventures, 1974.

Peterson, Frederick. *Ancient Mexico.* New York: Capricorn Books, 1959.

Pewe, Troy L. and Updike, Randall G. *San Francisco Peaks.* Museum of Northern Arizona, 1976.

Radbruch, Dorothy H.; Blanchard. F.B.; Bonilla, M.G.; Cluff, Lloyd S. *Tectonic Creep in the Hayward Fault Zone, California.* Washington, DC: Geological Survey Circular 525, 1966.

Ramsey, Jarold. *Coyote Was Going There: Indian Literature of Oregon.* Seattle: University of Washington Press, 1977.

Redfern, Ron. *The Making of a Continent.* New York: Times Books, 1983.

Rinehart, C. Dean and Smith, Ward C. *Earthquakes and Young Volcanoes.* Palo Alto, CA: Genny Smith Books, 1982.

Schnell, Mary L. and Herd, Darrell G. *National Earthquake Hazards Reduction Program: Report to the United States Congress.* Washington, DC: Geological Survey Circular 919, 1983.

Secor, R.J. *Mexico's Volcanoes.* Seattle: The Mountaineers, 1981.

Shane, Scott. *Discovering Mount St. Helens.* Seattle: University of Washington Press, 1985.

Sharp, Robert. *Southern California Geology Field Guide.* Dubuque, IA: Kendall/Hunt, 1975.

Sheets, Payson D. and Grayson, Donald K. *Volcanic Activity and Human Ecology.* Orlando, FL: Academic Press, 1979.

Simkin, Tom; Siebert, Lee; McClelland, Lindsay; et al. *Volcanoes of the World: A Regional Directory of Volcanism During the Last 10,000 Years.* Stroudsburg, PA: Hutchinson Ross Publishing Co., 1981.

Stanley, Mildred de. *The Salton Sea.* Los Angeles: Triumph Press, 1966.

Stearns, Harold T. *Geology of the State of Hawaii.* Palo Alto, CA: Pacific Books, 1966.

Stone, Scott C.S. *Volcano!!* Honolulu: Island Heritage, 1977.

Time-Life Books. *Volcano.* Alexandria, VA: 1982.

Tompkins, Peter. *Mysteries of the Mexican Pyramids.* New York: Harper & Row, 1976.

Uyeda, Seiya. *The New View of the Earth.* San Francisco: W.H. Freeman, 1971.

Walker, Bryce and the Editors of Time-Life Books. *Earthquake.* Alexandria, VA: Time-Life Books, 1982.

Wenkam, Robert. *The Great Pacific Ripoff.* Chicago: Follett, 1974.

————. *The Big Island Hawaii.* Chicago: Rand McNally, 1975.

Williams, Howel. *The Ancient Volcanoes of Oregon.* Eugene: Oregon State System of Higher Education, 1976.

Wilson, J. Tuzo. *Continents Adrift and Continents Aground.* San Francisco: W.H. Freeman, 1963–1976.

Wyllie, Peter J. *The Way the Earth Works.* New York: John Wiley, 1976.

Yandell, Michael D. *Yellowstone National Park.* Casper, WY: World-Wide Research and Publishing, 1976.

Yanev, Peter. *Peace of Mind in Earthquake Country.* San Francisco: Chronicle Books, 1974.

Yerkes, R.F.; Bonilla, M.G.; Youd, T.L.; Sims, J.D. *Geologic Environment of the Van Norman Reservoirs Area.* Washington, DC: Geological Survey Circular 691-A,B, 1974.